PRIVATE GARDENS

of the Potomac &
Chesapeake

CLAUDIA KOUSOULAS

FOREWORD BY ADRIAN HIGGINS

PRIVATE GARDENS
of the Potomac & Chesapeake

SCHIFFER PUBLISHING

4880 Lower Valley Road • Atglen, PA 19310

Other Schiffer Books on Related Subjects:

Regional Landscape Architecture: Northern California; Rooted in Resilience, Jeffrey Head, ISBN 978-0-7643-5835-7

Regional Landscape Architecture: Southern California; Mediterranean Modern, Jeffrey Head, ISBN 978-0-7643-5836-4

Designed by Molly Shields
Cover photo by Melissa Clark

Type set in Effra/Cambria
ISBN: 978-0-7643-6601-7
Printed in China

Published by Schiffer Publishing, Ltd.
4880 Lower Valley Road
Atglen, PA 19310
Phone: (610) 593-1777; Fax: (610) 593-2002
Email: Info@schifferbooks.com
Web: www.schifferbooks.com

For our complete selection of fine books on this and related subjects, please visit our website at www.schifferbooks.com. You may also write for a free catalog.

Schiffer Publishing's titles are available at special discounts for bulk purchases for sales promotions or premiums. Special editions, including personalized covers, corporate imprints, and excerpts, can be created in large quantities for special needs. For more information, contact the publisher.

MIX
Paper | Supporting responsible forestry
FSC® C104723

TO GARDENERS, WHO, WITH LABOR AND SKILL,
CARE FOR THE LAND AND OUR COMMUNITIES

CONTENTS

FOREWORD

The twentieth-century design luminary and landscape architect Sylvia Crowe, musing in the 1950s, seemed to be looking to our own febrile age when she wrote that gardens represent "a peaceful refuge in a noisy world."

That's what a private residential garden is, a contained and personal retreat. But creating one is not about escaping the world so much as greeting it on our own terms, to be with family and friends, to grow favorite plants, and to find solitude where we can reconnect with nature, even if that is an abstracted waterfall.

The gardens in this book are the creations of some of the most accomplished landscape architects working in the eastern United States, many whose work I have admired for decades.

Their designs here are given form by an array of builders, landscape firms, and artisans who are duly credited. There is a heroic quality to this collaboration, because a finished garden inherently veils the challenges and tribulations that go into making it. The designer is at the center of this web and must be not just an artist but an engineer, a hydrologist, an ecologist, a horticulturist, and, always, a psychologist.

This is all in the service of the clients, whose decision to turn to design practitioners of renown speaks to their sophistication as well.

There is a lot of talk today about providing gardens for beleaguered pollinators and other wildlife. This is a worthy ambition, and gardens rich in perennials will do this naturally, just as they will bring alive the dynamism of the seasons. But here is a radical thought: gardens are for people. That is the essence of this book.

As much as I love the new perennial garden, I am thrilled to see here examples of formal, pared-back gardens, whose strong lines and lucid spatial relationships convey a sense of harmony and serenity, two qualities in short supply today. And this studied minimalism does not negate mystery and revelation, as in Gregg Bleam's unfolding garden of three courtyards in historic Alexandria.

One aspect that elevates all these gardens is the avoidance of overwrought spaces for "outdoor living." Rather, they invite use by their refinement and character. These qualities are underscored by attention to detail and the choice of materials. I am delighted by the cedar perimeter fence at the contemporary suburban landscape by Lila Fendrick, where the horizontal boards become narrower at the top, a visual device that lightens its heft. In the same garden, the terrace grid of poured-in-place concrete is sublime.

At a small apartment building, a sunken, narrow courtyard designed by Jordan Loch transcends its function as a passage and rainwater collector and becomes an enchanting gathering place through, again, the innovative use of concrete and by keeping the plantings in scale.

The variety of gardens reminds us too that each must respond differently to its site and needs, but there is a shared vocabulary in the distinctive environment of this slice of the Mid-Atlantic region.

Here we experience an early spring; a long, steamy summer; and the glorious fall. The azure autumn skies turn paler in winter, but no less limpid, and soon enough that season's woodsmoke yields to cherry blossoms.

It is an environment that welcomes an enviably rich plant palette but also renders woody plants uncommonly lush. It always amazes me that a shade tree can attain after ten years or so in Washington a stature that would take twice as long elsewhere.

So if some of these gardens seem young, all the better to see their bones before they fill in. After the journey of creation comes the journey of growth and balance. A well-tempered garden lies somewhere between a work of art and an earthly paradise. Not a bad continuum to inhabit, or to draw your own inspiration from.

    —Adrian Higgins is the author of *Chanticleer: A Pleasure Garden* and the former longtime garden writer for the *Washington Post*.

INTRODUCTION

While the Capitol dome may be the center of the District of Columbia and its Maryland and Virginia suburbs, by geography and lifestyle the Capital region stretches to the Chesapeake Bay. Water runoff from suburban storm drains miles away eventually ends up in the bay, leading designers to consider sustainability and environment in both design and implementation. Residents of the region's urban and suburban communities use bay-area communities as waterfront escapes, and garden designers work with the Chesapeake's particular landscape—marsh, forest, and waterfront.

The region's gardens have a particular aesthetic shaped primarily by the plants that thrive in its climate. The Washington area's moderate climate allows designers to "borrow" plants from neighboring zones, north and south, test them to learn what thrives, and expand the palette.

That palette is also influenced by the area's long horticultural history. Colonial-era botanist and horticulturalist John Bartram established the nation's first botanical garden just outside Philadelphia, which became a library of native American plant species, including flowering trees and shrubs such as magnolia and serviceberry that contemporary designers call on for their shapes, colors, and fit in the environment.

In his research, Eric Groft of Oehme, van Sweden | OvS, discovered that at one time, Washington, DC, was a center for rose cultivation. More recently, he notes that "the Andre Viette Nursery has become a designer's mecca for perennial plants." Established on Long Island in 1929 and moved to Virginia in 1976, the Viette nursery has been hybridizing daylilies, phlox, peonies, and irises for generations.

In his classic book *The Potomac*, Frederick Gutheim describes the development of Washington houses after the Civil War, with their gardens, "a visible memento of the countryside brought to town." They were a place for favorite plants, a respite from the city's heat, a source of culinary and medicinal herbs, and a point of pride. This green pattern extended through the city, with row-house dooryard gardens and wide sidewalks fitted with planting boxes, a pattern that remains today.

Gutheim goes on to note that local crops—tobacco, wheat, and corn—were used in decorative building design, constituting a kind of "botanical architecture." The regional vernacular in architecture and garden design is inspired by the neoclassic design of Mount Vernon and Jefferson's gardens and home at Monticello. Their symmetrical spaces, red brick, and white-painted accents still appear in area gardens.

In their designs for these Capital region gardens—urban, suburban, and waterfront—the landscape architects incorporate environment and sustainability with aesthetics. Sustainability is a flexible term, and, in residential landscapes, it applies to construction decisions that protect the larger environment—whether incorporating erosion protection on waterfront sites or capturing and filtering rainwater on urban sites. Sustainability also applies to plant materials. All the designers are conscious of incorporating existing planting—such as the rare, native persimmon trees on Jordan Honeyman's Canal House site—but they also mix in native cultivars that support wildlife and are hardy enough to withstand unpredictable weather changes, from the shock of a cold winter to the ravages of a summer drought.

Sustainability also extends to the way homeowners live in and enjoy their gardens. As Kevin Campion says, everyone wants a low-maintenance garden these days. Traditional chemical-heavy lawns and persnickety rose beds are reconsidered. Lawns are not a default treatment, but carefully considered foregrounds or play areas. And roses are set aside in favor of plants that offer a year-round aesthetic—flowering in spring and summer but offering shape and texture in the winter.

In most of the featured designs, you'll see that the designers have created different zones—front and back yards serve different purposes and so are treated differently to mark public and private spaces. Program is everything, and in all cases, designers adjust expectations to serve the needs and preferences of their clients—whether creating two points of access at Lila Fendrick's design for a Suburban Residence or accommodating a young family's lifestyle as Jordan Loch does at East Street Garden.

The designers also consider structures and screening that integrate shoreline protection, water management, access, HVAC, and trash into the designs. These functions may be hidden but are still conveniently accessible and usable. It's an approach that makes a garden more functional and long lasting.

Many of these designers were called in during a house design or renovation and were involved in discussions of how the house will be sited or lived in. Entertaining calls for open and flexible spaces; a home office requires quiet space as a backdrop for work and focus. In all cases, they use materials that are of a piece with the structure and the environment to create a unified design. Fendrick's fence design echoes the house's lines and massing.

The designers are careful to choose the right plant for the right place but also use natives and pollinators that can support the surrounding environment. Jordan Honeyman has taken this approach to the utmost in their garden of natives that has drawn local wildlife, added to and tended by its owner.

Designers also consider climate. The Washington area swings between southern and northern climates, sometimes exceptionally wet or dry, and sometimes with harsh winters and hot summers. The humidity is a given; in fact, some of these gardens are best enjoyed not in the summer but in the mild seasons of autumn and spring. The mix of natives and cultivars has the benefit of being resilient in their environment, and also creating habitat for local bees, birds, and animals that further enlivens the gardens and connects them to the natural landscape.

All these designers seek to create four-season gardens. As Groft says, "Anyone can do spring," but the gardens here feature plant materials placed to create color and sculptural effects—the peeling birch bark of a single-stem river birch in the winter, the color of serviceberry trees in the fall. These are spaces that don't peak and fade but evolve through the year with a particular beauty in each season.

Time is part of the design. The ways plants grow and change over time is part of the designer's calculus, and nearly every project is given a second look after its first planting season to adjust materials and placement. Other projects have more-particular time strictures. At North Point, Loch Collective was on a deadline to have a planted site in time for a family celebration. Both OvS at Casa Luna and Moody Graham at Aberdeen Creek have had years-long relationships with the clients and the gardens, a perspective that allows for an unfolding of ideas.

The plant materials are arrayed differently in each garden, responding to site and style, but often to similar ends. Capturing and extending the natural surroundings creates a dialogue between nature's palette and the human hand. None of these gardens fall into landscape tropes—a lawn, a flower bed, a patio or deck with a grill or chaise. The designs here certainly accommodate an outdoor life of grilling and relaxation, but they also work with the particulars of the site and the considered preferences of the homeowner. Whether large or small, these designs maximize a site's potential, highlighting its features and creating an identity. Each garden becomes a unique conversation among sky, water, and land.

BROADWATER

ARNOLD, MARYLAND
Campion Hruby Landscape Architects

The DC-based owners of this garden wanted an escape from the city, and so they bought and renovated a small house and lot on the Magothy River in a community on the west side of the Chesapeake Bay. The getaway was so popular with their family that they decided to expand to the lot next door, where they sought to create a serene space, one focused on the long and deep view of the river.

The design of this modern enclave is grounded in three concepts—water, planes, and sculpture. These three ideas shape the design and function of the garden, from the small details of plant materials to the broader relationships among space, light, and activity.

Water is invisible, notes designer Kevin Campion, unless it interacts with light or is held in a vessel. This garden's first vessel is a channel along the front of the house that you step over to enter. It is a playful first reminder of the site's essence—its waterfront location on the river's shore-line. The garden's negative-edge pool with a river view is another vessel, this one acting as a mirror. The final vessel is the river itself, constantly changing with weather and season and thus changing the garden's mood.

As in all gardens, particularly waterfront ones and those seeking to be sustainable, managing water is part of the design. Broadwater's relationship with the river is an aesthetic but also a functional one. Water is captured off the roof and driveway in permeable pans, set into the earth and covered with pervious Mexican beach pebbles. It is then directed across a bridging lawn to a bioretention area planted with "wet feet" plants that create a Chesapeake tidal garden. Spartina and switchgrass hold and filter the water, cleaning it before it's released into the river.

At the house, the garden's arrangement of planes begins with the rectangular paving of the parking court, broken by strips of beach pebble. The house itself sits on a bluestone plinth that runs through the house and into the rear garden, shaping steps to a lawn that reaches down toward the river. That lawn becomes another plane. With their manicured surfaces edged by wild grasses, the terraced steps create a defined space between the house and the river.

From the house's entry to back garden's lawn, this garden design creates a setting for the house with folding and mirroring views of the landscape, house, and garden.

That juxtaposition of wild and manicured grass takes on a sculptural quality, particularly where a curved nautilus of grass rises into a green eddy edged with Corten steel. It's a sturdy kind of art, integral to the garden, part of its material. Closer to the river, a Corten steel screen is patterned to mimic the shapes created by light reflected on moving water. Set in front of the flickering light of a fire pit, the shapes morph and move, much like the river alongside.

The garden's strong sense of clarity and order is a framework for the shifting river and changing seasons that bring the garden a new mood every day throughout the year. A serene respite, but one that seems always new.

As with the driveway and parking court, paths are composed of slab pavers separated by permeable strips of Mexican beach pebbles and plants. This repeated pattern contrasts hard spaces and soft plantings at different scales, uniting the site design and supporting the environment.

PLANT LIST

TREES
Trident maple, *Acer buergerianum*
Silver maple, *Acer saccharinum*
River birch, *Betual nigra* 'Cully'
European hornbeam, *Carpinus betulus* 'Fastigiata'
Arborvitae, *Thuja* 'Green Giant'
Arborvitae, *Thuja* 'Emerald Green'
Willow oak, *Quercus phellos*

SHRUBS
Boxwood, *Buxus* ssp.
Panicle hydrangea, *Hydrangea paniculata* 'Limelight'
Red twig dogwood, *Cornus sericea* 'Baileyi'
Virginia sweetspire, *Itea virgininca* 'Little Henry'
Chesapeake Japanese holly, *Illex crenata* 'Chesapeake'
Arrowwood viburnum, *Viburnum dentatum* 'Blue Muffin'

PERENNIALS AND GRASSES
Butterfly weed, *Aesclepias tuberosa*
Drumstick allium, *Allium sphaerocphalon*
Giant allium, *Allium* 'Gladiator'
Coneflower, *Echineacea* 'Hot Papaya'
Bearded iris, *Iris germanica* 'Orange Harvest'
Northern blue flag iris, *Iris versicolor*
Cardinal flower, *Lobelia cardinalis*
Russian sage, *Salvia yangii* 'Little Spires'
May Night sage, *Salvia* 'May Night'
Rough goldenrod, *Solidago rugosa*
Scouring rush, *Equisetum hyemale*
Purple lovegrass, *Ergagrostis spectabilis*
Lily turf, *Ophiopogon*
Shenandoah switchgrass, *Panicum virgatum* 'Shenandoah'
Dwarf fountain grass, *Pennisetum alopecuroides* 'Hameln'
Autumn moor grass, *Sesleria autumnalis*
Giant feather grass, *Stipa gigantea*
Mexican feather grass, *Stipa tenuissima*

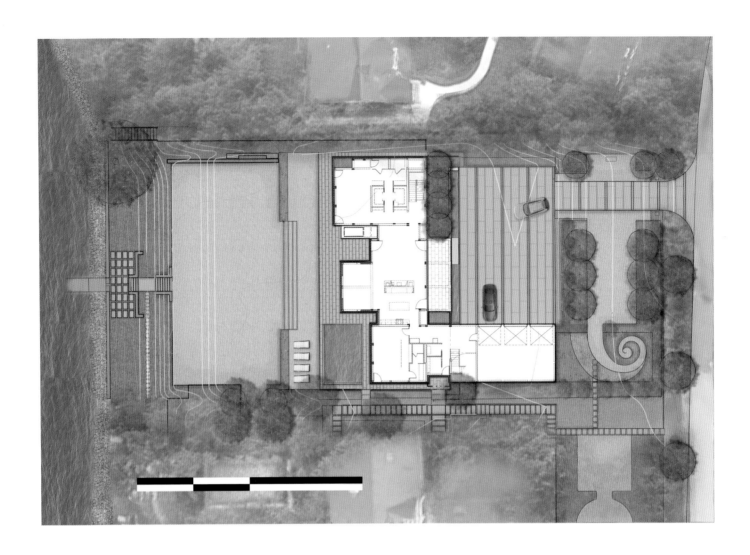

ARCHITECT: Alt Breeding Schwarz Architects
BUILDER: Pyramid Builders
INSTALLATION AND SUPPLIERS:
Evergro Landscaping
Walnut Hill Landscape Company
Gutierrez Studios (art, screens, gates)
Manuel Bartolo, Bartolo Ironworks (steel nautilus)
Hyde Concrete (driveway)
Terra Nova Design (irrigation/lighting)
Sunset Group (pool)
PHOTOGRAPHY: David Burroughs Photography

HAMPDEN LANE RESIDENCE

BETHESDA, MARYLAND
Campion Hruby Landscape Architects

At this new house in an established neighborhood, the owner sought to create more house on a smaller footprint, leaving room for intentionally designed gardens and outdoor space. To create a low-maintenance, contemporary-styled respite, Campion Hruby had to deal with clayey soils, poor drainage, and an aggressive stand of bamboo. The construction and installation called for remediating the soil, managing drainage, and blocking and removing the bamboo.

But beyond the functional requirements, Campion Hruby developed a design plan that created three spaces—an entry garden, a pool garden, and a garden deck in the back of the house. These spaces are defined with long bands of loose native grass that extend from the house like a pinwheel. The distinct spaces are further defined by stacked stone walls but are connected by ipe bridges that are lit from below and appear to float at night.

This mix of hard and soft, order and disorder, is a structuring device that the Campion Hruby designers return to in their work. They often use hardscape—walks, driveways, and decks or patios—to declare spaces that establish a design armature for the garden. Then they fill in with plants that vary in shape and color with a looseness and ease. At this property, the front garden is defined by the driveway and walkway with the spikes of 'Ice Dance' carex grass as a green background broken by thousands of spring-blooming bulbs, and summer alliums.

Designer Kevin Campion has observed that clients are "okay with some shagginess in the design." Most are not looking for ornate, high-maintenance gardens, but ones that have some natural disorder built in. The bands of *calamagrostis × acutiflora* 'Karl Foster' between each garden room create natural partitions.

The entry garden, including the driveway and walkway, is shaped as a series of parallel and perpendicular axes, edged with trident maples—a naturally small tree that won't overgrow the space and will provide brilliant fall color. The entry space is anchored with a water feature that draws visitors into the space with sound. The fountain is a stacked stone wall with scuppers dropping into a shallow, 12-inch-deep pool. The scuppers can be adjusted so that the sound of splashing water can be modulated and heard outside and inside the house.

In this garden, the juxtaposition of hard and soft, tight and loose, is visually interesting and easy to maintain. Plants are chosen to be unappetizing to deer but supportive of birds and insects, and they require a trim only once a year. In massed plantings, they create drifts of color and texture.

PLANT LIST

TREES
Arborvitae, *Arborvitae thuja* 'Green Emerald'
River birch, *Betula nigra* 'Heritage'
American hornbeam, *Carpinus caroliniana*
Trident maple, *Acer buergerianum* 'Ayem'

SHRUBS
Big-leaf hydrangea, *Hydrangea macrophylla* 'Endless Summer'
Panicle hydrangea, *Hydrangea paniculate* 'Limelight'
Virginia sweetspire, *Itea virginica*
Skip laurel, *Prunus laurocerasus* 'Schipkaensis'

PERENNIALS AND GRASSES
Hummingbird mint, *Agastche* 'Blue Fortune'
Lady fern, *Athyruym filix-femina*
Feather reed grass, *Calamagrostis acutiflora* 'Karl Forester'
Sedge, *Carex morrowii* 'Ice Dance'
Autumn fern, *Dryopteris erythrosora* 'Brilliance'
Coneflower, *Echinacea purpurea* 'Pow Wow White'
Purple lovegrass, *Eragrostis spectabilis*
Globe amaranth, *Gomphrena globose*
Lenten rose, *Helleborus hybridus* 'Blue Metallic Lady'
Giant alum root, *Huechera macrorhiza* 'Autumn Bride'
Bee balm, *Monarda didyma* 'Raspberry Wine'
Mexican feather grass, *Nassella tenuissima*
Mondo grass, *Ophiogon japonicus*
Cinnamon fern, *Osmunda cinnamomea*
Virginia creeper, *Parthenocissus tricuspidata* 'Variagated'
Fountain grass, *Pennisetum alopecuroides*
Fountain grass, *Pennisetum alopecuroides* 'Hameln'
Great Solomon's seal, *Polygonatum commutatum*
Christmas fern, *Polystichum acrostichoides*
Toad lily, *Trisyrtis hirta* 'Samurai'

The pool garden resolves a tricky geometry on a tight site. The rectangle is set within an oval space, leaving pockets of planting at the corners to soften the edges.

The rear deck is a private space for relaxing and entertaining, with a spa focused on a Corten steel fire pit that animates the space. Corten steel, also called weathering steel, rusts without corroding, a feature that makes it suitable for outdoor use and adds color and texture to a garden.

The plant palate is mostly native plants, such as monarda and false aster, that can draw urban wildlife and pollinators—including the fireflies that Campion remembers from his childhood.

This garden's puzzle pieces are carefully composed on a tight site. Fences, walls, and planting combine to create distinct spaces, views, and reflections. The centerpiece is the pool, serene and quiet, as well as a space for fun and gathering.

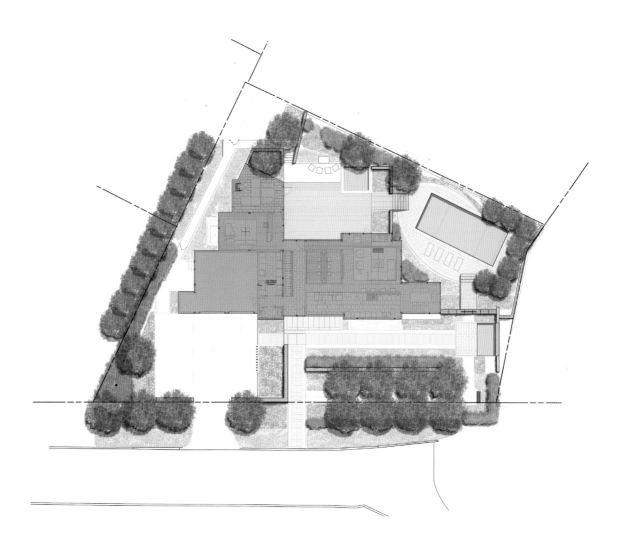

ARCHITECT: Robert M. Gurney, FAIA
BUILDER: Sandy Spring Builders (house, deck, pool, pool terrace, site walls, glass gates, driveway)
FOUNTAIN, PATHWAYS, FENCING: Kirk Berry, SCAPES (no longer in business)
INSTALLATION:
Planted Earth Landscaping
Grown to be Wild Nursery
Outdoor Illumination (lights)
Serra Stone (hardscape)
Alpine Pool & Design Corporation (pool)
PHOTOGRAPHY: David Burroughs Photography

ABERDEEN CREEK

ANNAPOLIS, MARYLAND
Moody Graham

When the owners renovated the house on this roughly 1-acre waterfront lot, they had dramatic ideas for remaking the landscape, recalls designer Jay Graham. And in the more than twelve years since he's been working with them, each phase has eased the garden in a different direction.

The owners believe in nature's healing power, which they've expressed through their charitable foundation work and in their own garden. One of their wishes was to enter the property through a grove of trees, which led Graham to create a gravel-chip-on-asphalt driveway that bends to the shape of the lot and is lined with pawpaw trees. Pawpaws are a native understory tree that grows in thickets, which quickly created the desired effect. "They flower in April, fruit in September, and give beautiful color in October," says Graham.

In the rear of the house, off to one side, the original pool garden had been designed as a traditional suburban backyard focal point with a deck and diving board. The diving board was removed and the pool has been resurfaced in a dark finish to reflect the wooded glade of delicate river birch that surrounds it. It is still a respite from the heat, but a calm spot for reflection too.

The design decisions in this garden are almost invisible, placing the natural environment of wood and water at the forefront. Winding paths, a quiet pool, a wooded glade offer small surprises in a living and changing environment.

The property is the work of two designers. Shin Abe of Zen Associates designed the Japanese garden behind and alongside the house. Its stone paths, carefully placed and pruned trees, water stream, and topography are an interpretation of the surrounding natural environment. "Japanese gardens are an interpretation of nature," Abe says. They are generally asymmetrical, with a strong focal point, and often have a story. The story of this garden reflects the Chesapeake Bay as it drops from the heights of the Delaware Water Gap to open into the bay's waters. A natural hill in the upper garden is planted in dwarf mondo grass that flows down a dry waterfall of boulders to a stone bridge crossing a sweeping pool of white stone.

This garden's edges are planted with Japanese cedar, native holly, black pine, Japanese maples, azaleas, and a centerpiece flowering cherry—a palette of seasonal color. Over time the trees and shrubs have been carefully pruned to develop an intricate branching pattern. Abe points out that Japanese gardens can be deceptively high maintenance. While the contrast of a carpet of fallen autumn leaves on the white stone is a seasonal gift, the casual debris that can accumulate draws away from the garden's artistry.

The two gardens work in harmony with each other and with the house. With time, the house and garden have been adapted to each other. A large floor-to-ceiling window

in the living room draws the garden into the house, and a small, 10-by-10-foot pocket garden is visible from the bedroom and office.

Paths from the Japanese garden lead to the creek front. "This was a rare situation where the owner didn't want the full view of the water," says Graham. The creek is narrow at that spot, and houses on the opposite bank are part of the view. Rather than having an open vista here, a planted path winds along the creek, permitting glimpses of the water and horizon, and small resting spaces lie along its route. The intention was to create a distinct place, and the path widens at its bend to accommodate a bench. A curved, dry-stacked stone wall runs along the hillside, adding definition to the path and edge and protecting the hill from erosion.

Each bit of the garden has been built from inspiration—the owners' and the designers'—over time. Sometimes the directions and planting have been very specific; at other times, a mention of desire or experience is enough to shape a design. A garden bench was inspired by the house's midcentury modern style and is modeled on a classic Parson's table. A temple bell brought home from travels is set into a stone arm, first sketched and then sculpted by Graham and turned over to a stonemason to be shaped out of bluestone. The wooden rail along the creek was built in phases from collected branches.

Over time, the garden has grown from shared visions and skills.

PLANT LIST

TREES
Pawpaw, *Asimina triloba*
Chinquapin, *Castanea pumila*
Japanese cedar, *Cryptomeria japonica*
Kaki persimmon, *Diospyrus kaki*
Foster holly, *Ilex fosterii*
American holly, *Ilex opaca*
Lacebark pine, *Pinus bungeana*
River birch, *Betula nigra* 'Little King'
River birch, *Betula nigra* 'Heritage'

SHRUBS
Bottlebrush buckeye, *Aesculus parviflora*
Red chokeberry, *Aronia arbutifolia* 'Brilliantissima'
Japanese camellia, *Camellia transnokoensis*
Dwarf fothergilla, *Fothergilla gardenii*
Witch-alder, *Fothergilla major*
Arnold Promise witchhazel, *Hamamelis* × *intermedia*
'Arnold Promise'
St. John's wort, *Hypericum* 'Hidcote'
Winterberry holly, *Ilex verticillata*
Inkberry holly, *Ilex glabra*
Virginia sweetspire, *Itea virginica*
False-holly, *Osmanthus heterophyllus* 'Rotundifolius'
Jostaberry, *Ribes grossularia* × *nigrum*
Clove currant, *Ribes odoratum*
Red currant, *Ribes sativum*
Lowbush blueberry, *Vaccinium angustifolium*
Highbush blueberry, *Vaccinium corymbosum*
Conoy viburnum, *Viburnum* × 'Conoy'

PERENNIALS AND GRASSES
Maidenhair fern, *Adiantum pedatum*
Columbine, *Aquilegia canadensis*
Lady fern, *Athyrium felix-femina*
Green and gold, *Chrysoganum virginianum*
Autumn fern, *Dryopteris erythrosora* 'Brilliance'
Barrenwort, *Epimedium* × *versicolor* 'Sulphureum'
Virginia strawberry, *Fragaria virginiana*
Wintergreen, *Gaultheria procumbens*
Cranesbill, *Geranium macrorrhizum*
Cranesbill, *Geranium maculatum*
Dwarf mondo grass, *Ophiopogon japonicus* 'Nana'
Cinnamon fern, *Osmunda cinnamomea*
Allegheny spurge, *Pachysandra procumbens*
Sherwood purple creeping phlox, *Phlox stolonifera*
'Sherwood Purple'
Mayapple, *Podophyllum peltatum*
Solomon's seal, *Polygonatum multiflorum*
Running tapestry foamflower, *Tiarella cordifolia*
'Running Tapestry'

Within the larger site, the Japanese garden interprets the natural environment. In the larger garden, design elements are inspired by the waterfront site. Paths slowly reveal views, encouraging a visitor to explore and discover. The groundskeeper, who is also a woodworker, created the fence and bench from salvaged wood.

BUILDER: Winchester Construction
GARDEN DESIGNER: Zen Associates
INSTALLATION: Evergro Landscaping, Winchester Construction
SUPPLIERS:
Ron Ammon, the groundskeeper, built the rustic railings and benches.
Tom Jasick, a local mason, built the stone walls, some of the stone
paths, and the stone support for the bell.
PHOTOGRAPHY: Allen Russ

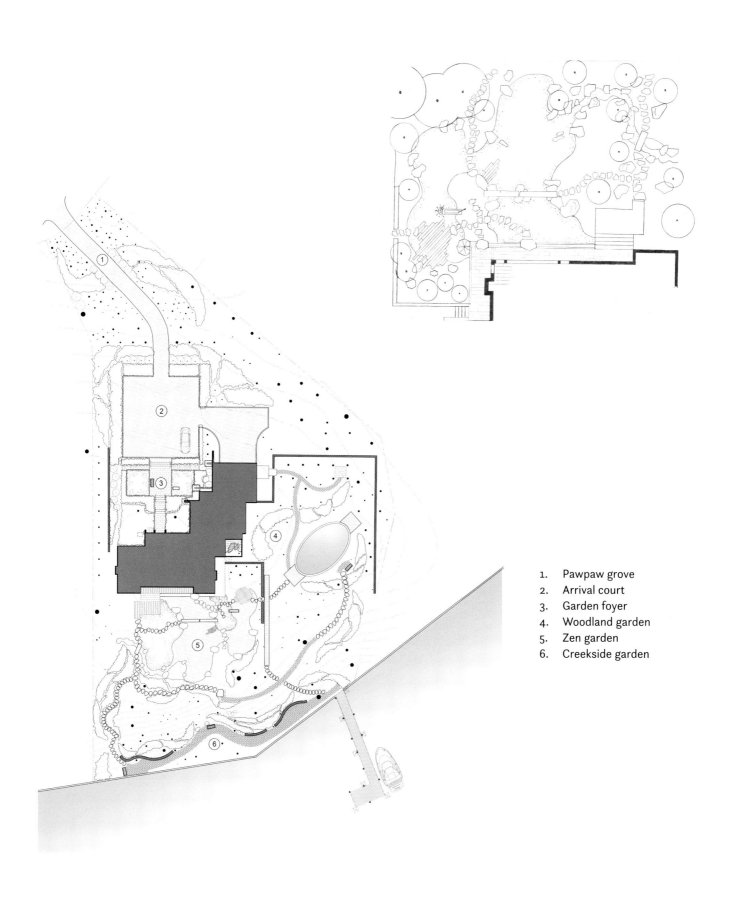

1. Pawpaw grove
2. Arrival court
3. Garden foyer
4. Woodland garden
5. Zen garden
6. Creekside garden

GARRETT PARK HOUSE

MONTGOMERY COUNTY, MARYLAND
Gregg Bleam Landscape Architect

This garden was created for a house in a historic streetcar suburb, developed in the 1890s to be accessible to downtown Washington by commuter train. The original house had burned down, leaving an open lot with close neighbors and little privacy.

Working with the owners, designer Gregg Bleam developed a garden program. Along with creating a sanctuary, it included creating a sustainable and low-maintenance house and landscape. "This is a neighborhood of narrow lots," says Bleam, "just 50 by 200 feet. Our goal was to max out the space and create a private garden."

The architect and landscape architect worked collaboratively, adjusting the foundation siting to design a window at the entry hall. The window created a visual link through the axis of the house, with a view from the entry to the backyard's garden and pool beyond.

The front of the house is treated as a contemporary take on a traditional front lawn. Although distinctive, it fits comfortably with its neighbors. The space is planted in a series of panels—vinca at the curb, a carpet of mondo grass beneath a redbud grove opening to a lawn.

On a narrow site and with a limited plant palette, this refined design creates spaces and shapes that are in conversation with the house. The pool, aligned with the entryway to the house, draws visitors into the garden.

The house's front door is reached via a bluestone path whose stones are equally spaced but set at a grade that makes them disappear into the lawn from eye level. The ribbon strip driveway from the street to the garage at the rear of the lot was both sustainable—it required less paving—and a nod to history and old-fashioned concrete-strip driveways. The parking area toward the front of the site is stabilized with grass pavers, minimizing the paving's appearance and maximizing its imperviousness.

The rear garden's minimalist form is anchored by a linear reflecting pool along the back of the house. While initially considering a swimming pool, the owners worked with Bleam on four schemes, eventually settling on a 6-inch-deep pool spanned by an ipe wood bridge. "There was a concern for safety," he recalls.

From the street front, through the house, into the back garden, this design creates a connected space composed of rectilinear beds, a pool, and paths, all shaped and enlivened by plant materials.

Instead of a pool, the owners' grandchildren can play on a long, parallel lawn. It is edged by a 12-foot-high European hornbeam hedge that has an almost architectural presence. Its columnar forms are neatly trimmed at the base, and their close planting creates a dense, green wall. The horsetail grass planted at the end of the pool is a water-friendly plant, and its feathery movements gives the illusion that the water continues. The grass's upright shape also mirrors the hornbeam hedge.

The hornbeam continues on the driveway side of the house, but rather than planting it as a wall parallel with the property line, the trees are planted perpendicular to the property line and driveway, shaping spaces that extend the house's view and sense of enclosure. They create a framework for three separate gardens that were left unplanted so that the client could choose to plant vegetables, perennials, or a cutting garden and create different plant palettes.

PLANT LIST

TREES
Serviceberry, *Amelanchier canadensis*
Redbud, *Cercis canadensis*
European hornbeam, *Carpinus betulus* 'Fastigiata'
Green giant arborvitae, *Thuja plicata* 'Green Giant'
Saucer magnolia 'Jane', *Magnolia soulangeana* 'Jane'

SHRUBS
Dwarf fothergilla, *Fothergilla gardenii*
Winterberry, *Ilex verticillata*

GRASSES
Scouring rush horsetail, *Equisetum hyemale*
Dwarf mondo grass, *Ophiogpogon japonicus* 'Nana'
Periwinkle, *Vinca minor*

Beyond the lawn and pool is a crushed-stone space planted with a bosk of serviceberry and anchored with a specimen magnolia. Its ipe wood bench picks up the color, material, and design of the bridge between lawn and house. Bleam notes that ipe is popular for its durability—it's tough and weathers well. The wood also has a reputation for sustainability, but locally grown black locust can be a good alternative and is easier to track from its source.

As a modern construction, this garden sits comfortably in its historic neighborhood by respecting the context. It works both for the clients and their neighbors.

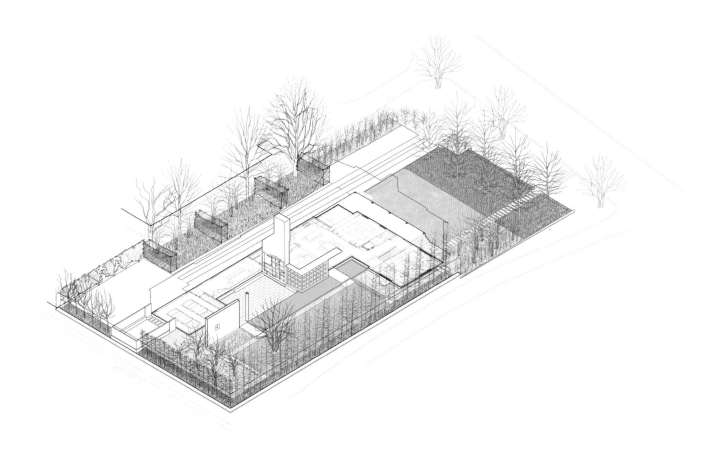

ARCHITECT: Richard Williams Architects
BUILDER: Alliance Builders
INSTALLATION: Evergro Landscaping
MATERIALS: Presto GeoSystems Invisible Structures,
Varicore Technologies
PHOTOGRAPHY: Scott F. Smith

OSLO ATLAS

WASHINGTON, DC
Loch Collective Landscape Architecture

The OSLO's developers describe this small apartment building as "an ideal alternative to a group house," a composition of multibedroom units designed to balance public and private space. Loch Collective's street-side landscaping and courtyard garden build on that concept. Set back along the street to align with its neighbors, the building's dooryard garden is a linear composition of ground cover and evergreen shrubs. These plantings screen the sunken infiltration pits that catch water runoff from the building and filter it through a variety of grasses.

At the building's entrance, a slatted wood screen and entry door also rises as a sheath around the internal staircase and becomes a privacy screen for the slightly below-grade courtyard garden. That garden receives sunlight through a large glass panel that also allows a view of the courtyard from the street. Through the season, two serviceberry trees, planted in a raised bed edged with an angled Corten steel frame, are visible from the street.

For this urban building, the garden adds
nature and value in a small space. In a
spot that might otherwise be overlooked,
simple interventions—seating, plank
flooring, and planting—create a shared
outdoor space for residents.

60

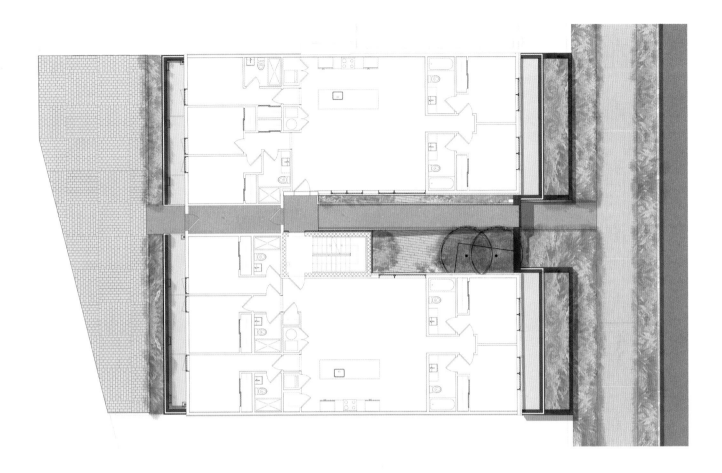

The sunken courtyard is a shared space, its design carefully considered to accommodate eight to ten people—enough for a small gathering, but not enough to become a potentially disruptive party space. The building's two below-grade units have direct access; they can leave their doors open to extend the units' shared living spaces into the garden, turning a potential drawback into an asset.

The courtyard is finished with plank-shaped concrete pavers placed at an angle to make the narrow space feel wider and create a feeling of movement through it. Part of the courtyard is covered by the gangway walk that leads

from the street to the building entrance, creating another space within a space.

The courtyard's location on the building's north side and its shallow planting beds—only about 8 inches—limited the choice of plant materials. Designer Jordan Loch developed a spreadsheet of plants that would work, which led to a plant palette of woodland grasses, shade-loving perennials, and an understory serviceberry tree, a native species whose white spring blossoms give way to brilliantly colored leaves in the fall.

PLANT LIST

TREES
Serviceberry, *Amelanchier canadensis*
Japanese boxwood, *Buxus microphylla* 'Morris Midget'

PERENNIALS AND GRASSES
White wood aster, *Aster divaricatus*
Lady fern, *Athyrium filix-femina*
Southern lady fern, *Athyrium filix-femina* ssp. *asplenoides*
Lenten rose, *Helleborus hybridus* 'White Lady'
Virginia bluebell, *Mertensia virginica*
Cinnamon fern, *Osmunda cinnamomea*
Appalachian sedge, *Carex Appalachia*
Bristleleaf sedge, *Carex eburnean*
Eastern star sedge, *Carex radiata*
Mondo grass, *Ophiopogon japonicus*
Shenandoah switchgrass, *Panicum virgatum* 'Shenandoah'
Autumn moor grass, *Sesleria autumnalis*

Along with navigating a tight space with many demands on it, the garden meets DC green-space regulations for minimal water use. The infiltration pits mediate among the garden's function, design, and experience.

The garden is also low maintenance, requiring only temporary irrigation with hand watering, cutting back the plants once a year, and occasional cleanups. With space for bike storage, the courtyard is well used and requires an annual refresh to keep it green and inviting. It is evidence that even in the most-unwelcoming spaces, gardens create both value and beauty.

The contrast of delicate blooms against a concrete wall catches the eye of a passerby. Just peeking over the wall and enclosed by a glass wall, the serviceberry becomes an artifact marking the building's entrance, no matter the season.

DITTO.

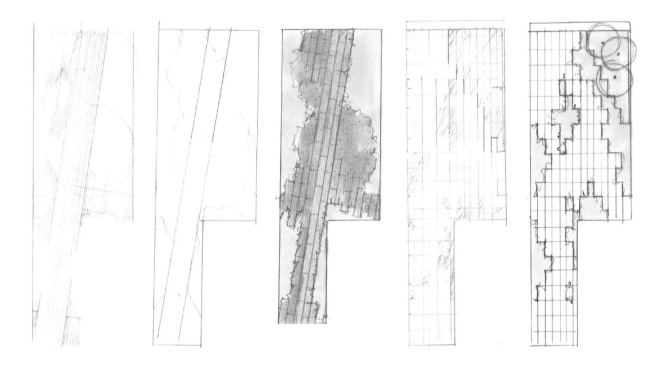

DEVELOPER: Ditto Development
ARCHITECT: Square 134, Loch Collective (facades/exterior)
BUILDER: Ditto Residential
NURSERIES:
Babikow Nurseries
Kurt Bluemel Nurseries
PHOTOGRAPHY: Jessica Marcotte, Kristian Zuniga / Loch Collective

SUBURBAN RESIDENCE

WASHINGTON, DC, METRO AREA
Lila Fendrick Landscape Architects

In many desirable neighborhoods, existing houses are being replaced by new construction, creating an opportunity to reconceive both the house and the landscape to accommodate modern lifestyles. The owners chose this lot because it is within walking distance of a nearby suburban downtown, and both the house and landscape accommodate their goals to age in place and continue to work in home offices.

The architect, the landscape architect (Lila Fendrick), and the owner collaborated on the program for the house and land, responding to the owners' particular requests. Parking areas for the family and the home offices were kept separate, to preserve privacy. The site was designed in zones to accommodate space for services such as trash and HVAC that would be screened but convenient. The design also includes a small butterfly garden to attract pollinators and support the owner's beekeeping hobby.

The overall goal, of course, was to create a harmonious fit with its neighbors, using existing setbacks and siting patterns while also achieving privacy for the house and yard on a corner lot.

Stepping away from the traditional suburban front yard of lawn and driveway, this design arranges intersections of lines and shapes to compose garden and house into a unified design. Materials— ipe wood and micro-etched concrete— are arrayed to define spaces.

The landscape design steps away from traditional suburban tropes of driveway and front walk to respond to how the couple want to live in their home. The corner lot affords the opportunity for two car courts—one for clients and one for the family. Likewise, instead of a symmetrical front walk typical of suburban lots, the entry to the house is via a jogged, stepped path from the sidewalk.

This suburban lawn is also used to create space and privacy. Not a large swath of green, but an intentional space for grandchildren to play within sight of the patio, made of etched concrete and river stone. The lawn of heat-resistant zoysia sod is easy to maintain and supported by an irrigation system. The lawn across the front and sides of the house is broken by a staggered laurel hedge that creates

a conceptual sense of enclosure and will grow into a continuous green wall. The hedge lines emphasize the jogged path to the front door, creating a delightful approach to the house and tucking the front walkway away from the sidewalk. In contrast to the home's sharp lines, loose and lush horsetail grasses soften a neighbor's stone wall and the edge of the entry path.

In the front garden, Fendrick added a weeping katsura, visible from a home office and at an oblique angle from the kitchen windows. It was set to create height in that corner of the garden, which lacked any tall vegetation. The tree also balances the existing large Japanese maple in the house's front corner.

A created view turns a dim functional space—a challenge—into a moment of serenity and even inspiration.

Patterns and materials connect the house and garden. The patio is reached through sliding doors in a window wall, creating a connected space in fine weather and a light-filled view on less clement days. The patio's grid lines, in an arrangement of poured-in-place concrete panels and beach pebbles, reflect the house's strong lines. The concrete is finished with a micro-etched surface that creates a fine texture and almost stonelike appearance, adding visual interest and friction to avoid a slippery surface.

Another opportunity to bring the outdoors inside is the garden space set in a below-grade window well. What might have otherwise been a blank and bleak view is made into a vitrine, displaying a statue on a custom pedestal in front of an ipe wall and planter of horsetail rush. It's an elegant arrangement of planes and materials that creates depth in a small space. "It was a challenge," Fendrick says, "but it means a lot to the owner."

This sort of attention to detail is typical of Fendrick's work. Repeated colors and materials create a unified design. The small pebbles used in the joints between the patio's etched concrete panels are echoed by the larger rounded beach pebbles in the stone strip that wraps the base of the house. To anchor the sleek look of the stucco brought to grade, this stone gutter keeps a clean base, catching water and

PLANT LIST

TREES
Weeping katsura, *Cercidiphyllum japonicum* forma *pendulum*

SHRUBS
Skip laurel, *Prunus laurocerasus* 'Schipkaensis'
Elkhorn cedar, *Thujopsis dolabrata*
Slender hinoki false cypress, *Chamaecyparis obtusa* 'Gracilis'

PERENNIALS AND GRASSES
Horsetail rush, *Equisetum hyemale*
Butterfly weed, *Asclepias tuberosa*
Milkweed, *Asclepias*
Obedient plant, *Physostegia virginiana*
Purple coneflower, *Echinacea*
White Japanese anemone, *Anemone hupehensis*
Verbena, *Verbena bonariensis*
Blue grama grass, *Bouteloua gracilis*
Sideoats grama grass, *Bouteloua curtipendula*

GROUND COVER
Zoysia sod
Big Blue liriope, *Liriope muscari* 'Big Blue'
Karl Foerster grass, *Calamagrostis* × *acutiflora* 'Karl Foerster'

eliminating the need to maintain foundation plantings. The downspout catchments create a linear composition with grates that keep them clear of debris.

The house's strong horizontal lines are reflected in the horizontal slats of the cedar wood fence that wraps the site, in what Fendrick calls one of the design's "big gestures." The fence helps unify the design and is stained to match the house's cedar siding and the color of two red maples and the existing Japanese maple. The fence's graduated slats reflect the house's rising vertical proportions with a broad base and more delicate top.

This garden is the result of collaboration and observation to develop a unified design—one that serves its owners and community.

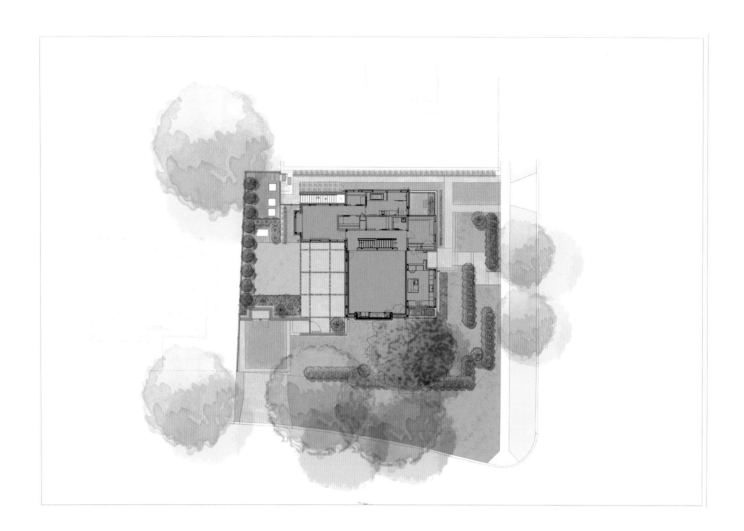

ARCHITECT: Wiedemann Architects
BUILDER: McNamara Brothers
LANDSCAPE CONTRACTOR: Evergro Landscaping
PHOTOGRAPHY: Hoachlander Davis Photography

CHAPMAN STABLES

WASHINGTON, DC
Clinton+Ries Landscape Architects

Washington is more than monuments and Victorian townhouses. Some of the most interesting spaces and places are created out of former industrial buildings that kept the city running behind the scenes.

The Chapman Stables condominium was developed out of the Chapman Coal Company stable and garage. This complex of light industrial buildings was originally constructed circa 1906 and evolved from a stable to a parking garage, later used as a warehouse. In its latest evolution, it is a place to live and enjoy a naturalized urban environment.

Clinton+Ries' work encompassed three spaces: the ground floor dooryards that provide a public profile, the interior courtyard shared by residents and visitors, and the rooftop deck and terraces that provide views and environmental function. The goal was to create a four-season garden that would introduce nature into an industrial and urban environment; to "bring a sense of the wild into the space," says designer Kate Ries.

The site comprises two buildings around a central courtyard—the original two-story brick stable building facing the street and a new five-story building on the lot's interior.

The historic building runs along N Street and the main entrance reaches out "like a tongue," into the brick sidewalk, says Ries. The path of reclaimed bricks with a distinct color and pattern travels through the lobby into the central courtyard between the old and new building, drawing the street into the garden.

Street-facing units are entered through their own small gardens. In Washington, these planted dooryards, often behind an ornamental iron fence, are a traditional pattern. Here the bluestone-paved dooryards are planted with loose and billowy natives behind black wrought iron fencing. The bluestone complements the red brick, and although the fences are traditional, the plants are not the usual clipped boxwood. The bright purple flowers and

dusty green leaves of catmint, and rambling double-knock-out roses, lend spots of color and overall movement that soften the urban environment of brick and iron. Even though the façade doesn't share the street's repeated townhouse pattern, the historic building fits in through its setback and the dooryard plantings. The alley-facing units have dooryard gardens, too, their plants chosen to thrive in the shade.

The interior courtyard planting establishes the meadow theme, focused on a central planter of Corten steel that shapes the walkways between the buildings. The courtyard is built "on structure," and its beds and drainage are designed to accommodate the parking garage below grade. Clinton+Ries were part of the design team at the initial

In this renovated building, found space on rooftop decks enhances the wide views, softens the urban landscape, and performs an environmental function as green roofs. As a building amenity, the shared and private green spaces are true luxury.

Balance and differentiation, evident in detail decisions and material choice—reclaimed brick and wrought-iron fencing—create a street front that is harmonious but distinct. The brick is laid in a herringbone pattern to mark the building entrance, carrying through to the courtyard garden.

stages, which allowed the courtyard garden to be designed with deeper beds to accommodate trees, and to navigate the grade changes required by the site.

The central planter and the surrounding beds of massed plants—ligularia, liatris, echinacea—extend the meadow theme, and three fountains at the east end bring in the sound of trickling water. The overall arrangement creates a diagonal path through the courtyard, drawing users through the garden, but still creating a direct route. The whole composition is designed to be viewed from the units above and to be an extension of the ground floor units' gardens.

Upper-floor units also have outside space—individual terraces separated by small, planted areas and surrounded by green roof. The luxury of deep beds wasn't possible on the roof, so, Ries says, they set the usual sedum mats and

inter-planted them with perennials and grasses that would thrive in the 8 inches of soil. Ries points out that it was an approach that kept costs down, met the city's requirement for native plants, and created the textured, four-season garden that mimics the ground plane's design. "Panicum grass will get 3 feet tall, so that gave some height." Beyond the private spaces, an amenity deck offers seating, socializing, and views to the city skyline and the Capitol dome.

Within the project's complexity, from structure to design, attention to detail creates a curated and comfortable environment. Plant materials introduce a wild nature into the urban environment, the dooryard design complements the neighboring streetscape, and even a feature like the courtyard's gabion wall composed of wire and river stones recalls the building's industrial history.

PLANT LIST

TREES
Dura Heat river birch, *Betula nigra* 'Dura Heat'
Shademaster honeylocust, *Gleditsia triacanthos inermis* 'Shademaster'
Yellowwood, *Cladrastis kentukea*
Flowering dogwood, *Cornus florida*
Arnold Promise witch hazel, *Hamamelis × intermedia* 'Arnold Promise'
Sweetbay magnolia, *Magnolia virginiana*
Snowbell, *Styrax japonicus*
Drake's Chinese elm, *Ulmus parvifolia* 'Drake'

SHRUBS
Sawtooth Japanese aucuba, *Aucuba japonica* 'Serratifolia'
Shamrock holly, *Ilex glabra* 'Shamrock'
Leatherleaf mahonia, *Mahonia bealei*
Heavenly bamboo, *Nandina domestica* 'Obsession'
Heavenly bamboo, *Nandina domestica*
P.J.M. rhododendron, *Rhododendron × 'P.J.M.'*
Double knockout rose, *Rosa × 'Radrazz'*

PERENNIALS, GROUND COVERS, AND GRASSES
Moonshine yarrow, *Achillea × 'Moonshine'*
Bugbane, *Actaea simplex* 'Hillside Black Beauty'
Blue giant hyssop, *Agastache foeniculum*
Black Scallop bugleweed, *Ajuga reptans* 'Black Scallop'
Purple Sensation ornamental onion, *Allium aflatunense* 'Purple Sensation'
Forescate chives, *Allium schoenoprasum* 'Forescate'
Purple sensation allium, *Allium sphaerocephalon* 'Drumstick'
Butterfly weed, *Asclepias tuberosa*
Wonder of Staffa aster, *Aster × frikartii* 'Wonder of Staffa'
Deutschland astilbe, *Astilbe × arendsii* 'Deutschland'
Blonde Ambition blue gamma grass, *Bouteloua gracilis* 'Blonde Ambition'
Feather reed grass, *Calamagrostis × acutiflora* 'Karl Foerster'
Reed grass, *Calamagrostis × acutiflora* 'Overdam'
Reed grass, *Calamagrostis brachytricha*
Slim-stem reed grass, *Calamagrostis stricta*

Japanese sedge, *Carex oshimensis* 'Everillo'
Threadleaf coreopsis, *Coreopsis verticillata* 'Moon Beam'
Threadleaf coreopsis, *Coreopsis verticillata* 'Zagreb'
Carthusian pink, *Dianthus carthusianorum*
Purple lovegrass, *Eragrostis spectabilis*
Blanket flower, *Gaillardia aristata* 'Lucky Wheeler'
Rozanne geranium, *Geranium* 'Gerwat'
Ingwersen's Variety cranesbill, *Geranium macrorrhizum* 'Ingwersen's Variety'
Japanese forest grass, *Hakonechloa macra* 'Aureola'
Japanese forest grass, *Hakonechloa macra*
Whitelady hellebore, *Helleborus × hybridus* 'White Lady'
Daylily, *Hemerocalis* 'Stella de oro'
Green Spice heuchera, *Heuchera* 'Green Spice'
Blue Angel hosta, *Hosta* 'Blue Angel'
Blazing star, *Liatris spicata*
Leopard plant, *Ligularia denata* 'Desdemona'
Big Blue lilyturf, *Liriope muscari* 'Big Blue'
Creeping Jenny, *Lysimachia nummularia* 'Aurea'
Scarlet Cambridge bergamont, *Monarda didyma* 'Scarlet Cambridge'
Pink muhly grass, *Muhlenbergia capillaris*
Walker's Low catmint, *Nepeta faassenii* 'Walker's Low'
Kent Beauty ornamental oregano, *Origanum* 'Kent Beauty'
Haense Herms witchgrass, *Panicum virgatum* 'Haense Herms'
Heavy Metal switchgrass, *Panicum virgatum* 'Heavy Metal'
Fountain grass, *Pennisetum alopecuroides*
Russian sage, *Perovskia atriplicifolia*
Firetail mountainfleece, *Persicaria amplexicaulis* 'Firetail'
Solomon's seal, *Polygonatum odoratum* 'Variegatum'
Black-eyed Susan, *Rudbeckia fulgida × fulgida*
Black-eyed Susan, *Rudbeckia hirta*
East Friesland salvia, *Salvia nemorosa* 'East Friesland'
Stonecrop sedum, *Sedum* 'Autumn Joy'
Prairie dropseed, *Sporobolus heterolepis* 'Tara'
Trumpet honeysuckle, *Lonicera sempervirens* 'Major Wheeler'
Boston ivy, *Parthenocissus tricuspidata* 'Veitchii'

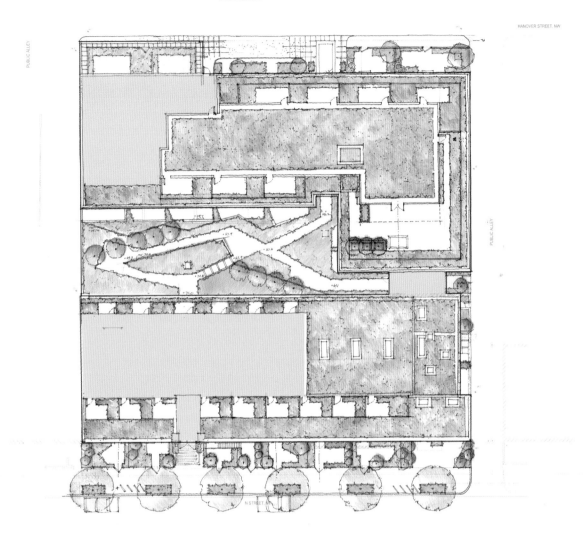

DEVELOPER: Four Points
ARCHITECT: Studio Twenty Seven Architecture
BUILDER: GCS|SIGAL (formerly Sigal Construction)
LANDSCAPE CONTRACTOR: Complete Landscaping Service
NURSERIES: Perennial Farm, Ingleside Plantation
Nurseries, Johnson Farms, Cavanos Perennials
GREEN ROOF: Columbia Green Technologies
IRON FENCING: Jerith Manufacturing Company
FOUNTAIN: Campania International
PHOTOGRAPHY: Sandra Clinton, Xing Chen (C+RLA)

CANAL HOUSE

NORTH SHORES
Jordan Honeyman Landscape Architecture

Delaware beaches are a weekend and summer escape for many in the Capital region, but more than just beaches, they are a varied natural environment of seafront, canals, marshes, and forest.

This property, on the Intracoastal Canal, is coastal maritime forest with sandy soil, facing a grassy marsh and perennial wetlands. Buildings in these wetland areas have to meet various state regulations for shoreline construction; for example, houses must be sited above the high tide line. Permit applications must also include a water drainage plan. On this site, designer Holt Jordan used perforated pipes that distribute water across the site's sandy soil and permeable surfaces, which include crushed clamshell paving for the driveway and paths.

Jordan, the architect, and the owner drew up their own goals: the landscape plan would highlight views across the canal to the marshes; it would include plants that attract pollinators, and there would be no lawn or chemical maintenance. The design of the house and garden evolved together, with lots of early collaboration between the three of them.

An organizing design feature is the continuous boardwalk path from the street front, along the house, to the canal waterfront. The path connects the varied outdoor spaces created by the integrated design of house and landscape—from screened and open porches to deck and dock.

Jordan recalls the decision to pull the deck away from the house and set it floating amid a stand of existing native persimmon trees. "The trees have a distinctive bark that adds year-round visual interest, and they're hard to replant, so it made sense to leave them in place," he says. The deck's cutouts accommodate the trees' growth. Other strategic design choices provided energy-saving shading for the house.

At a finer scale, the garden is composed of a range of native plants mixed with some exotics, chosen for summer color and all-season interest. Cultivars of Joe Pye weed, golden-rod, and milkweed are bred for color, shape, size, and their "good behavior"; they won't spread the way a straight species would. Massed along the canal front and along the path to the dock, they create a parterre effect, their wild shapes held in check in beds. This multispecies garden attracts birds and butterflies. "It is not a sterile environment," Jordan says.

"The first year was a struggle," he adds. Some plants were lost to deer, and supplemental plants were added. As the garden has settled in, further adjustments have enhanced the views from the house and its outdoor spaces, anchoring it as a composition of building and garden in nature.

As the zoned design moves through varied outdoor spaces—the house's deck and screened porch, stone walkways, dock, and water—the materials and plants change to mark space and respond to the environment.

The garden's design is a careful integration of natural and constructed environments. The view is paramount, but plants were chosen to be adaptable to the waterfront climate. The existing native persimmon trees, with their distinctive bark, are hard to replant, so the deck was designed around them.

PLANT LIST

TREES
London plane tree, *Platanus acerifolia*
Sycamore, *Platanus occidentalis*
American persimmon, *Diospyros virginiana*

SHRUBS
Beach plum, *Prunus maritima*
Black myrtle, *Myrtus communis*
Winterberry holly, *Ilex verticillata*
Sumac, *Rhus* spp.

PERENNIALS AND GRASSES
Geranium 'Rozanne'
Catnip, *Nepeta cataria*
Bee balm, *Monarda didyma*
Switchgrass, *Panicum virgatum*
Muhly grass, *Muhlbergia*
Little bluestar, *Amsonia tabernaemontana*
Milkweed, *Asclepias syriaca*
Goldenrod, *Solidago*
Joe Pye weed, *Eutrochium purpureum*
Yarrow, *Achillea millefolium*
Evening primrose, *Oenothera*
Summer sweet, *Clethra alnifolia*
Bottle brush, *Callistemon*

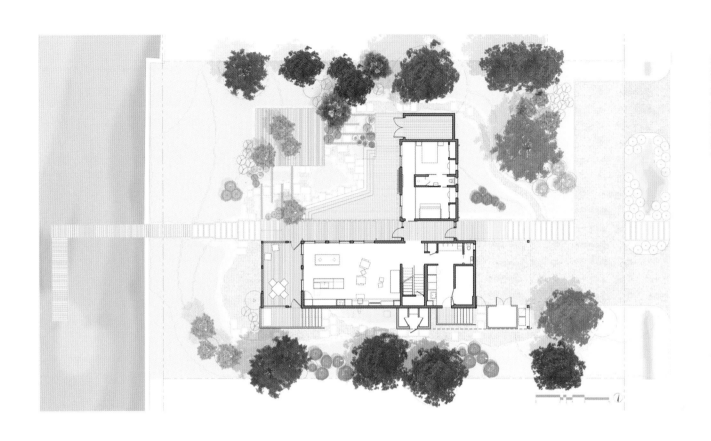

ARCHITECT: Gardner Architects
BUILDER: Beachwood Custom Builders
INSTALLER: Bella Terra Landscapes
PHOTOGRAPHY: John Cole

EAST STREET GARDEN

ANNAPOLIS, MARYLAND
Loch Collective

Dating to the 1700s, this house and its site reflected eras of change. Designer Jordan Loch Crabtree recalls that site work revealed evidence of an outhouse and horses, as well as its former use as an auto body shop. This renovation of house and garden was an opportunity to restore some dignity to the house and garden, on the brick sidewalk of a narrow street in the Maryland capital city's historic district.

The owners, a young family, looked to their garden as a respite and family space. They wanted active space for their children and room to host family meals as well as larger gatherings with friends—even an occasional dinner party or outdoor movie night.

Before the design could be expressed and refined, they had to resolve a serious drainage issue—water was coming into the home. The house's foundation is constructed of granite blocks used as ship's ballast. Though historic, and a charming story for the house tour, the stones were set with porous mortar. About 12 tons of soil were excavated, regraded, and amended to drain rainwater away from the house and replenish the groundwater. Rainwater that lands

in the garden perks into the soil or moves toward an infiltration basin sited below the children's river-pebble play
basin. Most of the water running off the roof moves directly
into the infiltration basin.

Other site issues were easier to manage with design solu-
tions, and Loch used materials and forms to create a modern
space in a historic envelope. The unattractive concrete
block wall at the rear of the lot was given a parge coat; its
fresco texture and color complements the house and creates
an accent wall in the garden. It also doubles as a projection
surface for outdoor movie nights. Well-worn fencing was
replaced by a tall fence of narrow vertical slats. It steps
down at the street and echoes the slim trunks of the river
birches planted on the garden's west side.

On a small urban site, this multifunctional
garden is a family space and an extension
of their life in the house, with spaces for
play and entertaining. A garden wall
doubles as a movie screen, and boulders
and hand-hewn logs work for seating and
climbing. The design fits into the historic
neighborhood, using a tree on the lot next
door as a design feature.

The space itself uses historical patterns in a composition that meets the design goals. The square lawn, seen in other historic houses, is enclosed by a hedge, a lush planting of ferns, and a tall bed of grasses. It transitions into the river-pebble play basin, which shifts to a gravel patio along the house, similar to ones seen at Annapolis's historic St. John's College. The composition of lawn, stone, and gravel is punctuated by boulders set at varied heights. "We set them as they occur in nature, with the lichen above grade," says Loch. In conversation with the boulders, hunks of reclaimed white oak were hand-finished to create seating.

In this downtown neighborhood, neighbors are nearby, a feature Loch incorporated into the garden design. Working with the neighbor, the redbud next door was trimmed to accent the river birch, as does an adjacent mulberry. "Mulberry trees are found all over Annapolis," Loch says, "and this one provides a green backdrop."

PLANT LIST

TREES
Single-stem river birch, *Betula nigra*

PERENNIALS AND GRASSES
Karl Foerster reed grass, *Calamagrostis* 'Karl Foerster'
Wood fern, *Dryopteris marginalis*
Cinnamon fern, *Osmunda cinnamomea*

MATERIALS
Wood: solid white oak, reclaimed from highway construction
Stone: western Maryland Appalachian stone

RAINWATER TO GROUNDWATER

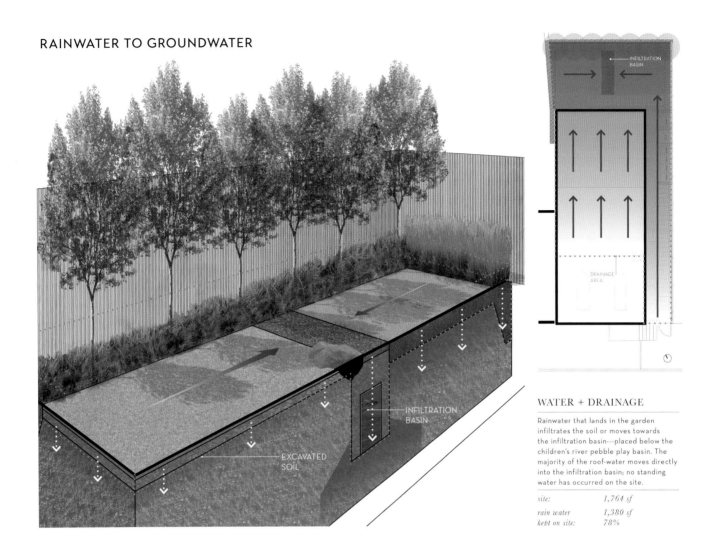

INFILTRATION
BASIN

DRAINAGE
AREA

EXCAVATED
SOIL

INFILTRATION
BASIN

WATER + DRAINAGE

Rainwater that lands in the garden
infiltrates the soil or moves towards
the infiltration basin---placed below the
children's river pebble play basin. The
majority of the roof-water moves directly
into the infiltration basin; no standing
water has occurred on the site.

site:	1,764 sf
rain water	1,380 sf
kept on site:	78%

LANDSCAPE CONTRACTOR: Solidago Landscapes
EXCAVATION: Planted Earth Landscaping
SAWYER: Seneca Creek Joinery
STONE YARD: Harwood Stone
PHOTOGRAPHY: Anchor Pictures / Mason Summers

CASTING A VISION FOR THE GARDEN

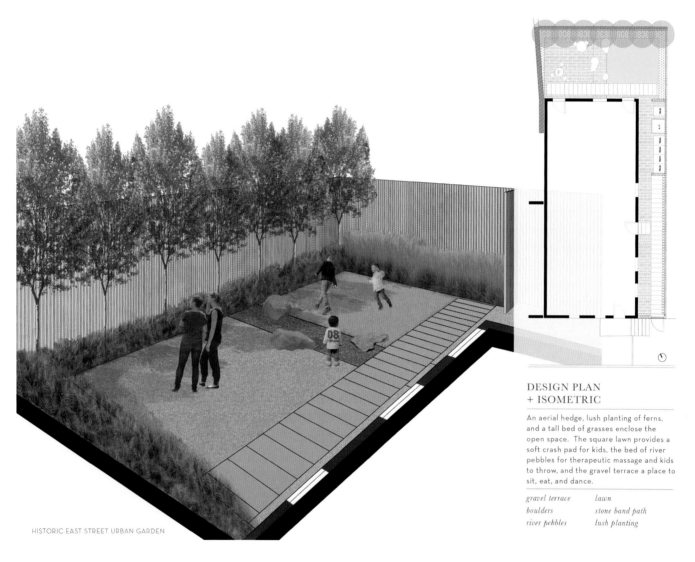

HISTORIC EAST STREET URBAN GARDEN

DESIGN PLAN + ISOMETRIC

An aerial hedge, lush planting of ferns, and a tall bed of grasses enclose the open space. The square lawn provides a soft crash pad for kids, the bed of river pebbles for therapeutic massage and kids to throw, and the gravel terrace a place to sit, eat, and dance.

gravel terrace   *lawn*
boulders   *stone band path*
river pebbles   *lush planting*

CLIENT DESIRES

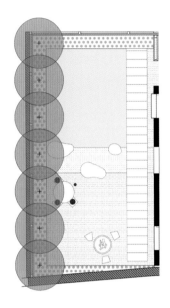

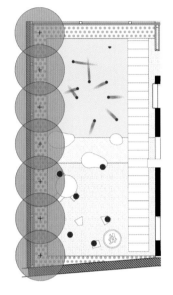

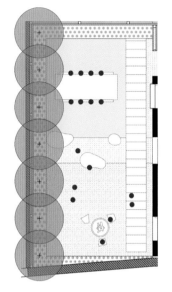

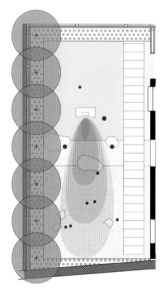

FAMILY
MEALS

people:	2 adults + 2 kids
frequency:	2x day
needs:	cafe table

FAMILY + FRIEND
GATHERINGS

people:	6 - 8 adults + 4 - 8 kids
frequency:	1x week
needs:	cafe table
	fire feature
	open lawn

COCKTAIL + DINNER
PARTY

people:	8 - 12 adults
frequency:	2x month
needs:	dining table
	fire feature

MOVIE
NIGHT

people:	6 - 8 adults + 4 - 8 kids
frequency:	1x week
needs:	fire feature
	open lawn

HISTORIC EAST STREET URBAN GARDEN

TAYLOR RESIDENCE

FALLS CHURCH, VIRGINIA
Jordan Honeyman Landscape Architecture

This ¾-acre garden and house cover two lots in suburban Virginia, just outside Washington, DC. When the owners bought the second plot, it contained a large pond designed by noted landscape architect Lester Albertson Collins. Jordan Honeyman reconfigured the pond so that it is smaller, more manageable, and integrated with the new design and habitat.

While the original pond was lined with cedar logs, the new koi pond is constructed with a rubber liner and edged with large boulders, which help it blend into the surrounding landscape. The new design also added a fountain and stream that meanders through the garden and contributes to its primary goal—to create habitat. The pond is edged with plants—sedge, wild celery, water lily, and others—that protect the fish from predators and attract birds and pollinators. The pond's ipe wood bridge is a focal point, connecting with a terrace at the house and a simple seating lawn. Movement through the landscape occurs on meandering paths that mirror the stream's path as it spills into the pond from a Corten steel fountain near the potting shed.

Arrayed over two house lots, this garden
stretches out with a design that accom-
modates both manicured and loose
spaces. A series of small environments,
each with a distinct function and
character, are connected with winding
paths and consistent materials.

Extensive plantings include trees, shrubs, ground covers, and vines that are composed to create layers of native and adaptive plants. The garden has become a sanctuary for wildlife, attracting bees, butterflies, and birds, including a heron. The firm often mixes native plants with adaptive plants—those that grow well in the area and won't become invasive—as a way to introduce variations in color, shape and size. As designer Holt Jordan notes, "Natives aren't always as ornamental or may not last as long." For example, Little Lime hydrangea's blooms begin in midsummer and last into fall, and the plant can handle drought as well as heavy rains.

Managing water is a key feature of the garden, and drainage structures are as layered as the plants. A large bioretention area planted with native species collects rainwater from ground surface runoff and roof drains. The water is directed into cistern storage, filtered through three layers of gravel, and slowly released into the public stormwater system. The design also takes opportunities to disperse water throughout the site, rather than directing it via gutters to a single location. The paths and driveway are paved with permeable materials—pavers and crushed gravel—that provide visual interest and allow more water to percolate into the soil.

Since its construction, the garden has grown into itself. Holt notes, "The homeowner is an avid gardener and is always making adjustments. Her commitment to it, always asking questions, is a beautiful thing to see."

Over time, the garden has grown into itself, with plants filling in beds and lining paths, drawing pollinators, and developing into a small but complex ecosystem. The garden's flexible design ensures it is an ongoing project for the owner, who adds plants every season.

PLANT LIST

TREES
Japanese maple, *Acer palmatum* 'Bloodgood'
Serviceberry, *Amelanchier canadensis* 'Autumn Brilliance'
River birch, *Betula nigra* 'Duraheat'
Eastern red cedar, *Juniperus virginiana*
Southern magnolia, *Magnolia grandiflora* 'Bracken's Brown Beauty'
Dwarf southern magnolia, *Magnolia grandiflora* 'Little Gem'
Apple, *Malus pumila* 'Stark Grand Gala'
Apple, *Malus pumila* 'Stark Super Red Fuji'
Chaste tree, *Vitex agnus-castus*

SHRUBS
Bottlebrush buckeye, *Aesculus parviflora*
Red chokeberry, *Aronia arbutifolia* 'Brilliantissima'
Slender deutzia, *Deutzia gracilis* 'Nikko'
Smooth hydrangea, *Hydrangea arborescens* 'Annabelle'
Hydrangea, *Hydrangea paniculata* 'Limelight'
Dwarf hydrangea, *Hydrangea paniculata* 'Little Lime'
Oakleaf hydrangea, *Hydrangea quercifolia* 'Pee Wee'
Oakleaf hydrangea, *Hydrangea quercifolia* 'Snow Queen'
Inkberry, *Ilex glabra*
Winterberry, *Ilex verticillata* 'Red Sprite'
Winterberry, *Ilex verticillata* 'Southern Gentleman'
Winterberry, *Ilex verticillata* 'Sparkleberry'
Virginia sweetspire, *Itea virginica* 'Little Henry'
Luykens laurel, *Prunus laurocerasus* 'Otto Luyken'
Fragrant sumac, *Rhus aromatica* 'Gro-Low'
Icy drift rose, *Rosa* × 'Icy Drift'
Dwarf blueberry, *Vaccinium caespitosum*
Indian summer viburnum, *Viburnum dentatum* 'Indian Summer'
Brandywine viburnum, *Viburnum nudum* 'Brandywine'
Smooth witherod, *Viburnum nudum* 'Winterthur'
Conoy viburnum, *Viburnum* × *burkwoodii* 'Conoy'
Alleghany viburnum, *Viburnum* × *rhytidophylloides* 'Alleghany'

VINES AND ESPALIER
Honeysuckle, *Lonicera* × *heckrottii* 'Gold Flame'
Virginia creeper, *Parthenocissus quinquefolia* 'Silver Vein'
Rose, *Rosa* × 'Graham Thomas'

GROUND COVER
Arkansas bluestar, *Amsonia hubrichtii*
Blue ice star flower, *Amsonia tabernaemontana* 'Blue Ice'
Anemone, *Anemone* × *hybrida* 'Honorine Jobert'
Butterfly milkweed, *Asclepias tuberosa*
Dwarf butterfly bush, *Buddleja davidii* 'Blue Chip'
Gold dew tufted hair grass, *Deschampsia cespitosa* 'Goldtau'
Autumn fern, *Dryopteris erythrosora* 'Brilliance'
Purple coneflower, *Echinacea purpurea* 'Ruby Star'
White coneflower, *Echinacea purpurea* 'White Swan'
Globe thistle, *Echinops bannaticus* 'Blue Glow'
Bicolor barrenwort, *Epimedium* × *versicolor* 'Sulphureum'
Spotted Joe Pye weed, *Eupatorium purpureum maculatum* 'Gateway'
Joe Pye weed, *Eupatorium* × 'Baby Joe'
Hybrid cranesbill, *Geranium* × 'Rozanne'
Big Blue lilyturf, *Liriope muscari* 'Big Blue'
Creeping mazus, *Mazus reptans*
Red bee balm, *Monarda* × 'Cambridge Scarlet'
Pink muhly grass, *Muhlenbergia capillaris*
Walkers Low catmint, *Nepeta* × *faassenii* 'Walkers Low'
Shenandoah switchgrass, *Panicum virgatum* 'Shenandoah'
Mountain mint, *Pycnanthemum virginianum*
Black-eyed Susan, *Rudbeckia fulgida sullivantii* 'Goldsturm'
Matrona sedum, *Sedum telephium* 'Matrona'
Narrowleaf blue-eyed grass, *Sisyrinchium angustifolium*
Shade-tolerant sod

POND PLANTING
Golden tufted sedge, *Carex elata*
Siberian iris, *Iris sibirica* 'Caesar`s Brother'
Parrot feather, *Myriophyllum aquaticum*
Fragrant water lily, *Nymphaea odorata*
Pickerel weed, *Pontederia cordata*
Wild celery, *Vallisneria americana*

This project's extensive plant selection is arrayed in a layered composition of color, shape, and texture. Natives and native cultivars are chosen to be hardy through the seasons and to create a wildlife habitat for birds and insects.

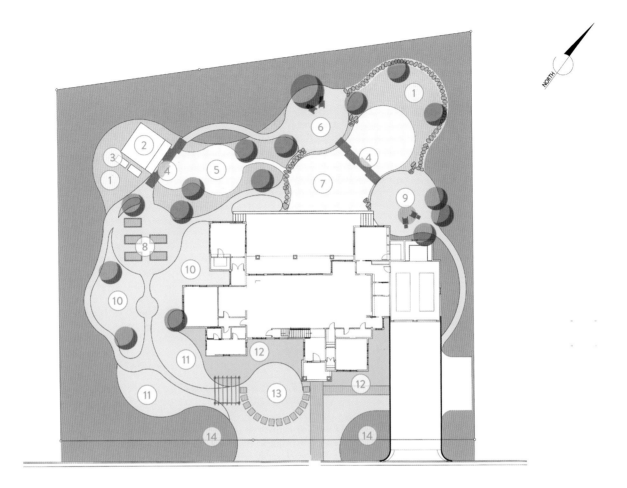

1   Wetland edge
2   Greenhouse
3   Cold frames
4   Boardwalk
5   Bioretention wetland
6   Clearing in lawn
7   Wetland (pond)
8   Vegetable beds
9   Clearing in lawn (mulched seating area)
10 Meadow
11 Meadow berm
12 Garden
13 Lawn
14 Forest

ARCHITECT: Moore Architects
BUILDER: Ironstar Building Company
LANDSCAPE CONTRACTOR: GROW Landscapes
POND CONTRACTOR: Harmony Ponds
PHOTOGRAPHY: Melissa Clark

3303 WATER STREET

WASHINGTON, DC
Oehme | van Sweden

Although Georgetown is known as an elegant and historic neighborhood, its waterfront was the site of warehouses, canal boat landings, and industrial uses since the city's founding. Even through modern times, the waterfront was not an aesthetic asset but a functional one—a good location for a Pepco electrical substation and the Whitehurst Freeway, which threads along the river and into Maryland. Eventually, the brick warehouses and factories were transformed into office and residential uses, but the Pepco substation remains. The 3303 Water Street condominium, wrapping around the substation, would have left residents with a grim view of gravel rooftop and freeway.

The project's developer had purchased air rights to build on top of the substation, but mitigating the electromagnetic field was cost prohibitive. Instead, Eastbanc and Pepco worked cooperatively to create one of the region's first and most extensive green roofs. Designer Lisa Delplace recalls eighteen months of meetings, working with the structural engineer, and researching plant materials to reassure Pepco that a green roof wouldn't threaten the integrity of the roof membrane or the building's structure.

Like any successful garden design, this one considered both engineering and aesthetics. But as one of the earliest and most-extensive green roofs, the project needed to determine what the structure could accommodate as well as plant materials that would thrive on the rooftop and fulfill the design goals.

Delplace recalls that while there were European precedents, at the time there were few American green roofs. The extensive research for this project helped inform future work on green roofs. It also created a long-lived, abstract, meadow-style garden that turned a liability into an asset for residents and the surrounding buildings.

The substation roof could sustain the garden's weight and allowed for an 8-inch planting bed. That deeper bed could accommodate more than the usual shallow-rooted sedums. OvS chose a palette of resilient, woody plants inspired by the American prairie, which adapted their root systems to a more horizontal environment and thrived over time. Points on the roof over structural columns could take even more weight and allowed a deeper planting bed that accommodated shrubs and small trees.

The result is a garden designed in two planes, in a parterre pattern for residents on the upper floors and as a view across the Potomac for residents on lower floors. Delplace imagined the space as a painting, with the roof's parapet walls acting as a frame within which the plants create bold and abstract blocks of color. Even in this unusual and harsh environment, OvS applied its approach of layered plantings that create shifting and evolving colors, volumes, and shapes through the seasons. Daffodils, in this deep soil, will naturalize and spread a carpet of color in the spring, then settle down as the summer grasses rise and change the rooftop meadow's profile.

The planted roof has environmental benefits—capturing and filtering stormwater and slowing its release, and mitigating urban heat islands—but it also creates beauty in a less-than-ideal environment. In fact, the garden has become popular with migratory birds—a good nesting spot, with no predators. Delplace says that many residents were fascinated by the unanticipated wildlife and even bought binoculars. Of course, birds carry the seeds of invasive plants and weeds that initially intruded on the garden's planting, but, says Delplace, as caretakers came to distinguish between intentional and opportunistic plants, the garden has thrived.

Beyond the rooftop, the project addressed private terraces on the first floor. They are designed with a trellis system that incorporates scuppers directing rainwater to a drain in the parking garage. The tall screens of wire mesh were applied in a contrapuntal, Mondrian-inspired pattern that functions as a composition, one that becomes even more complex as vines fill in the panels with a varied green pattern.

The project's complexity shows the value of research, returning to the site for observation, and the benefits of taking a bold step.

PLANT LIST

GROUND-LEVEL TREES
River birch, *Betula nigra*
White crape myrtle, *Lagerstroemia indica* 'Natchez'
Sweetbay magnolia, *Magnolia virginiana*

GROUND-LEVEL SHRUBS
Black chokeberry, *Aronia melenocarpa*
Dwarf fothergilla, *Fothergilla gardenii*
Oakleaf hydrangea, *Hydrangea quercifolia*
Winter jasmine, *Jasminum nudiflorum*
Heavenly bamboo, *Nandina domestica*
Heavenly bamboo, *Nandina* 'Plum Passion'
Exbury azalea, *Rhododendron* 'Exbury Hybrids'
Sweetbox, *Sarcococca hookerana*
Spreading English yew, *Taxus baccata* 'Repandens'

GROUND-LEVEL PERENNIALS AND GRASSES
Monkshood, *Aconitum carmichaelii*
Lady's mantle, *Alchemilla mollis*
Pink Japanese anemone, *Anemone hupehensis* 'September Charm'
Goatsbeard, *Aruncus* 'Kneiffi'
Dwarf light-purple false spirea, *Astilbe chinensis* 'Pumila'
Pink false spirea, *Astilbe chinensis* 'Finale'
False spirea, *Astilbe* var. *davidii*
White false spirea, *Astilbe japonica* 'Deutschland'
Siberian bugloss, *Brunnera macrophylla*
Light-pink bigroot geranium, *Geranium macrorrhizum* 'Spessart'
Hardy geranium, *Geranium cantabrigiense* × 'Karmina'
Lenten rose, *Helleborus orientalis*
Plantain lily, *Hosta* 'Big Daddy'
Plantain lily, *Hosta* 'Sum & Substance'
Aaron's beard / St. John's wort, *Hypericum calycinum*

Lilyturf, *Liriope muscari* 'Big Blue'
Yellow spikes, *Ligularia stenocephala* 'The Rocket'
Christmas fern, *Polystichum acrostichoides*
Ostrich fern, *Matteuccia pensylvanica*
Fiveleaf akebia, *Akebia quinata*
Jackman clematis, *Clematis* × *jackmanii*
Sweet autumn clematis, *Clematis paniculata*
Blue clump bamboo, *Fargesia nitida*
Hakone grass, *Hakonechloa macra*
Variegated hakone grass, *Hakonechloa macra* 'Aureola'

ROOFTOP GARDEN SHRUBS
Chaste tree, *Vitex agnus-castus* 'Silver Spire'
Pink rose, *Rosa* 'Nearly Wild'

ROOFTOP PERENNIALS AND GRASSES
Red yarrow, *Achillea millefolium* 'Terra Cotta'
Giant ornamental onion, *Allium giganteum*
Boltonia, *Boltonia asteroides*
Bluebeard, *Caryopteris* × *clandonensis* 'Longwood Blue'
Daylily, *Hemerocallis* spp.
Gayfeather, *Liatris* 'Kobold'
Russian sage, *Perovskia atriplicifolia*
Black-eyed Susan, *Rudbeckia fulgida* 'Goldsturm'
Autumn Joy stonecrop, *Sedum* × 'Autumn Joy'
Stonecrop, *Sedum* × 'Robustum'
Little bluestem, *Andropogon scoparius* 'The Blues'
Feather reed grass, *Calamagrostis* × *acutiflora* 'Karl Foerster'
Red maiden grass / flame grass, *Miscanthus purpurascens*
Wind's Game tall purple moor grass, *Molinia littoralis* 'Windspiel'
Fountain grass, *Pennisetum alopecuroides*

Even in a limited space and limited capacity, the design achieves the expansiveness and seasonal beauty of a wild meadow. The designer treated both the roof and walls like a canvas, establishing a form and painting it with color and texture.

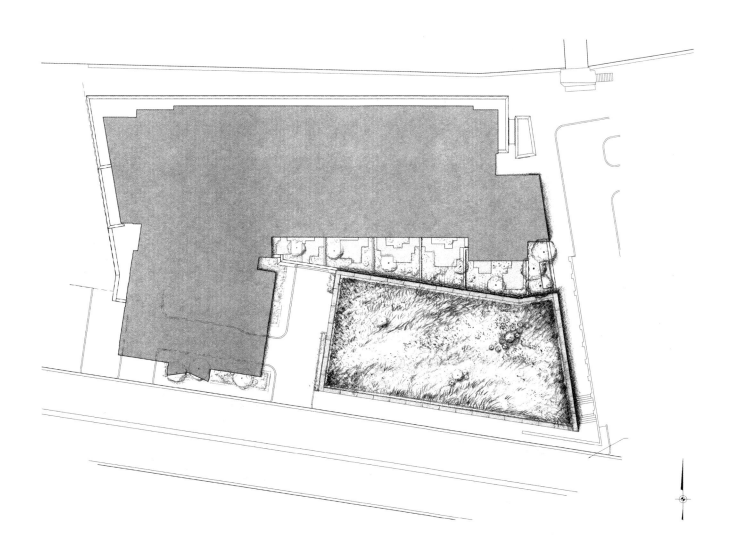

ARCHITECT: Handel Architects, with Frank Schlesinger Associates
DEVELOPER: EastBanc
CONTRACTOR: Clark Construction
INSTALLERS: Chapel Valley Landscaping

3 COURTYARDS

ALEXANDRIA, VIRGINIA
Gregg Bleam Landscape Architect

This small compound of residential buildings in the historic Alexandria neighborhood is linked by gardens that create privacy and related but distinct spaces. "The idea was to create three gardens, each with a unique treatment of water to connect the house and garden spaces," says landscape architect Gregg Bleam.

The site comprises the L-shaped main house and a separate guesthouse. Gardens are arranged and landscaped to create privacy from the street and connected spaces, each with a different function and feel. Each space fits into the historical tradition of courtyards and formal gardens, but all are finished with a refined modernism composed of shapes and materials that echo and repeat.

The house wraps around the largest garden—a rectangular space, centered on a pool edged with a bluestone sill and set amid a lawn defined by layered yew and holly hedges. This north-side garden is an extension of the living room. Bleam recalls that the pool evolved from a fountain to a water feature and finally to a spa pool. "We worked with the pool designer to make the pool a visual feature." Its black finish reflects the sky, and the pool equipment is hidden behind a freestanding bronze wall incised with a grid pattern. The composition is a modern take on the symmetry of a historical formal garden.

At the back of the house, the south entry garden is a long rectangular space where the owners will pull out a table to host dinner parties. An ipe bench on bronze supports runs along the original white-columned pergola, draped in wisteria. Between its columns, Bleam set three bronze planters filled with billows of laurel. Here, the slab-shaped bluestone pavers are tightly laid, creating a smooth surface, but with set lines that lead the eye to two bronze tanks at the far end—one planted with the upright spikes of scouring rush horsetail and the other containing a subtle fountain that drops water through a comb filter into a small basin, creating a delicate background sound.

The west garden flows between the main house and the guesthouse and repeats similar shapes and materials, but arranged differently. Here, the bluestone slabs that replaced the original brick paving are set farther apart, creating a distinct pattern broken by a negative-edge bronze water tank that sheets water into a trough. The brick walls are planted with Virginia creeper and climbing hydrangea to soften the space.

With a tightly curated palette and attention to how spaces are used, the design injects a historic property with serene modernism.

The refinement of a colonial garden is
reinterpreted here with a contemporary
palette—defined planting areas, water
features, and functional spaces—using
complementary building and plant materials.

PLANT LIST

NORTH COURTYARD
Hick's yew, *Taxus × media* 'Hicksii'
American boxwood, *Buxus sempervirens*
Shadblow serviceberry trees, *Amelanchier canadensis*
Boston ivy, *Parthenocissus tricuspidata*
White-flowering periwinkle, *Vinca minor* 'Alba'

SOUTH GARDEN
Scouring rush horsetail, *Equisetum hyemale*
(fountain tank)
Otto Luyken laurel, *Prunus laurocerasus* 'Otto Luyken'
Autumn crocus, *Crocus speciousus*
Spring crocus, *Crocus vernus*
Snowdrop, *Galanthus elwesii*
Christmas fern, *Polystichum acrostichoides*
Dwarf crested iris, *Iris cristata*
Japanese maple, *Acer japonica* (existing)
Wisteria (existing, on the pergola)

WEST GARDEN
Blackhaw viburnum, *Viburnum prunifolium*
Winterberry, *Ilex verticillata*
Dwarf fothergilla, *Fothergilla gardenii*
Edible white grape, *Villard blanc*
Climbing hydrangea, *Decumaria barbara*
Virginia creeper, *Parthenocissus quinquefolia*
Christmas fern, *Polystichum acrostichoides*
Canadian wild ginger, *Asarum canadense*
Autumn crocus, *Crocus speciousus*
Spring crocus, *Crocus vernus*
Snowdrop, *Galanthus elwesii*
Baltic ivy, *Hedera helix* 'Baltica'
Common periwinkle, *Vinca minor*

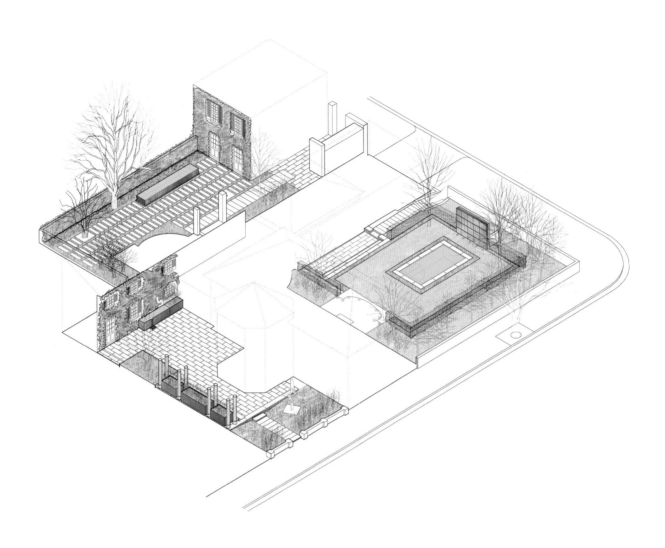

BUILDER: H. Gray Builders, Bonitt Builders
INSTALLATION: Evergro Landscaping
POOL DESIGNER: Alpine Pool & Design Corporation
METAL FABRICATOR (fountains and screen wall): Charles Yeager,
Yeager Design/Fabrication
PHOTOGRAPHY: Scott F. Smith

NORTH POINT

TRED AVON RIVER, EASTON, MARYLAND
Loch Collective

This project—a house under construction and its garden—had an unusual set of circumstances and a lovely reason for the accelerated schedule. The architects, a young couple, designed the house for one of their parents and planned to get married in the garden.

Loch Collective joined the design team in February and the wedding was scheduled for October, so there was no time to lose. And although the house was 75 percent complete when the landscape architecture firm arrived on the scene—much later than ideal—the architects had thought carefully about the house's relationship to the land, and the blended teams hit the ground running.

The 2.5-acre property on Maryland's Eastern Shore was carved out of a larger estate that had been subdivided into waterfront lots. The plan was to replace a small, old cottage with a contemporary home set in an entertaining-worthy garden designed around the river frontage.

An existing long driveway ended in a circle at the house, a traditional Eastern Shore gesture. To strengthen its relationship to the entrance, Jordan Loch pulled the circle into an ellipse shape. New grading created a platform

Bold geometries and careful siting shape
the garden's overall design and its
details, with plant materials used to
highlight shapes, spaces, and paths.

144

mound that sets the house up and off-center. The angled ellipse is planted with native grasses, perennials, and river birch to screen the entrance to the house. In conversation with the curved drive and ellipse, a gravel path establishes a strong design line through the site. It's paved in stone as it approaches the front courtyard and then moves through the home and out onto the pool deck and lawn. "It's an element that draws the eye into the landscape," Loch says. From that central axis, paths move at angles through various meadow spaces. "The entire site is wrapped in meadow," he says.

Replacing turfgrass with a meadow typically takes two to three years. Loch fast-tracked the process by designing two custom seed mixes. They prepped the site in July and planted in September, and a meadow of colorful annuals bloomed for the October wedding. The second mix is a long-term blend of natives designed to fill in the property over time.

Materials will weather naturally as the landscape matures. Arcing panels of Corten steel cut through the graded mound at the entry, echoing a hedgerow and enclosing the path to the house. The ipe pool deck is surrounded by a bluestone terrace and is raised about 30 inches, bringing the river into view.

The trees required particular attention. Working with an arborist, Loch surveyed the trees along the riverfront for health and species to meet county limits for removal and replacement within 100 feet of the river. They found that seven trees were completely covered in ivy and that others were invasive species. Nine trees were removed, opening the view and creating a healthy environment for the remaining trees.

At the house's entry, some trees were trimmed to improve their shape and health, and the mound was planted with single-stem river birch, a species native to floodplains and other wet environments. The single-stem variety has a sculptural shape, and here they create a scrim effect. River birch is a fast-growing species, and its peeling bark adds winter interest and highlights the tree's sculptural shape.

As on any property, but particularly on waterfront land, managing drainage and runoff is the key to environmental health. The landscape design incorporates large areas for infiltration. Rainwater is directed from downspouts to the meadow and planting beds, which are graded to move water gradually across the site and away from the river.

No doubt, every point in the design evokes a memory not only of its creation, but also celebration.

The site is wrapped in a meadow, a profile that creates a grassy enclosure within the site's treed enclosure. The design keeps views open, defines garden spaces, and blends into the waterfront landscape.

PLANT LIST

TREES
Single-stem river birch, *Betula nigra*

SHRUBS
Green Giant arborvitae, *Thuja* 'Green Giant'
Skip laurel, *Prunus laurocerasus* 'Schipkaensis'

PERENNIALS AND GRASSES
Giant hyssop, *Agastache* 'Black Adder'
Bluestar, *Amsonia hubrichtii*
Showy aster, *Aster spectabilis*
Lady fern, *Athyrium angustum* forma *rubellum*
Purple coneflower, *Echinacea purpurea* 'Magnus'
White coneflower, *Echinacea purpurea* 'Pow Wow White'
Ostrich fern, *Matteuccia struthiopteris*
Cinnamon fern, *Osmunda cinnamomea*
Russian sage, *Perovskia atriplicifolia* 'Little Spire'
Feather reed grass, *Calamagrostis* × *acutiflora* 'Karl
Foerster' tufted sedge, *Carex elata*
Horsetail, *Equisetum hyemale*
Mexican feather grass, *Nassella tenuissima*
Fountain grass, *Pennisetum alopecuroides* 'Hameln'
Northwind switchgrass, *Panicum virginiatum*
'Northwind'
Autumn moor grass, *Sesleria autumnalis*

ARCHITECT: Martins Grehl Architects
BUILDER: THINK MAKE BUILD
CONTRACTOR: Solidago Landscapes
NURSERIES:
Ernst Seed Company
Babikow Nurseries
Kurt Bluemel Nurseries
Manorview Farms
PHOTOGRAPHY: Anchor Pictures / Mason Summers

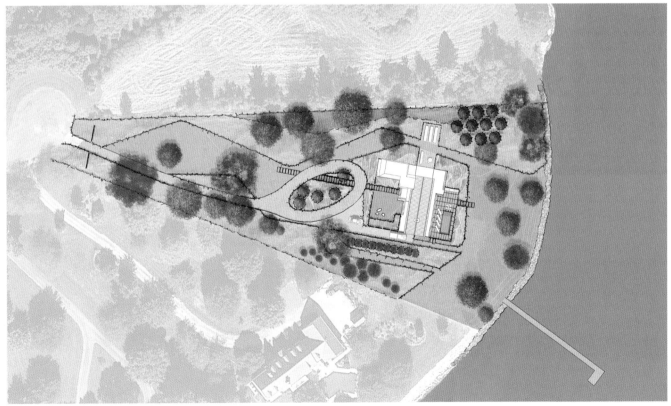

CASA LUNA

MARYLAND EASTERN SHORE
Oehme | van Sweden

It's not unusual for OvS to have decades-long relationships with clients as their gardens evolve. Casa Luna, an example of this partnership, is the third garden they developed at Halcyon, an 85-acre riverfront estate on Maryland's Eastern Shore. Firmly anchored in its environment, this structured garden was designed for the more modern of the two houses.

The first step was to meet state waterfront setback requirements, but also to stabilize the shoreline with stone groins and piers. Their hard edges were banked with water plants, and the severe structures are softened by an edge of grasses, creating a composition that holds and enhances the shoreline.

Casa Luna's design was shaped by the owner's desire to make it feel like a Georgetown garden—contained and carefully detailed. At the rear of the house, a small swimming pool is tucked against a low wall, which establishes an intimate space while hiding the mechanics of water circulation. A sheet of water cascades from the wall and onto bathers below. This is a refuge that melds easily with nature.

This garden's soft modernism carves a formal space out of the larger landscape, with sharply defined spaces set amid existing trees. Native plants link the garden to the natural setting.

Given the site's environmental sensitivity, care was taken to develop a planting plan that seamlessly integrates into the existing ecology. Tolerant of the salt air and marine clay, the planting plan infuses the landscape with color, texture, fragrance, and movement. It highlights the property's responses to changes in light, wind, and season, mimicking the ecological systems of the coastal meadow and contributing to the region's complex biodiversity. Layered masses of shrubs, grasses, and flowering herbaceous plants give the property an intimate feel and conceal a series of surprises.

Footpaths wander through a meadow, capitalizing on vistas over the water and dissolving into hidden destinations. A concrete pad, long a part of the landscape, was kept in place to serve as the foundation for an untitled Ben Forgey Jr. driftwood sculpture—stalks of foraged wood that mark

the corners, creating a minimalist enclosure with a distinct sense of space and a view to the river. Found materials further link the spaces to the environment.

All the plants at Casa Luna are natives—a choice that supports sustainability, but one that OvS had notably pursued in their work before sustainability was a design approach. Limiting lawn and "choosing the right plant for the right place," says designer Eric Groft, can create a place of intensity and drama, even in a small space.

This property's gardens are four-season environments—from the lush profusion of summer to the lean architecture of winter. "Anyone can do spring, with bulbs and color," says Groft. The challenge is to create a garden that doesn't peak but evolves—over seasons, but also over time.

Beyond the house, the garden expands into the landscape in a determined arrangement of native plants and found materials that maintain and enhance the natural environment.

PLANT LIST

TREES
Serviceberry, *Amelanchier canadensis*
Purple crape myrtle, *Lagerstroemia indica*
Southern magnolia, *Magnolia grandiflora*
Willow oak, *Quercus phellos*

SHRUBS
Inkberry holly, *Ilex glabra*
Southern wax-myrtle, *Myrica cerifera*
Conoy viburnum, *Viburnum × conoy*

PERENNIALS AND GRASSES
Swamp milkweed, *Asclepias incarnata*
Butterfly weed, *Asclepias tuberosa*
Blue aster, *Aster oblongifolius* 'October Skies'
Hemp agrimony, *Eupatorium cannabinum*
Joe-Pye weed, *Eupatorium fistulosum*
Hyssop-leaved thoroughwort, *Eupatorium hyssopifolium*
Rose mallow, *Hibiscus moscheutos* spp. *moscheutos*
Russian sage, *Salvia yanii*
Mountain mint, *Pycnanthemum muticum*
Great coneflower, *Rudbeckia maxima*
Purple spiderwort, *Tradescantia × *'Concord Grape'
Bowman's root / Culver's root, *Veronicastrum virginicum* 'Lavendelturm'
Feather reed grass, *Calamagrostis × acutiflora* 'Karl Foerster'
Wolfgang's palm sedge, *Carex muskingumensis* 'Oehme'
Wild oats, *Chasmanthium latifolium* (also *Uniola latifolia*)
Wind's Games tall purple moor grass, *Molinia litorialis* 'Windspiel'
Red switchgrass, *Panicum virgatum* 'Haense Herms'
Blue switchgrass, *Panicum virgatum* 'Northwind'
Little blue stem, *Schizachyrium scoparium* (also *Andropogon scoparius*)

Photography: Claire Takacs

APOTHEOSIS FARM

MARYLAND EASTERN SHORE
South Fork Studio

Residential gardens are often designed as frames or forecourts for the houses they surround, but this Eastern Shore garden exists as a small paradise carved out of a farm field.

The goal, says designer Miles Barnard, was to create privacy and surprise. "You don't see what's there until you open the gate," he says. The nineteenth-century historic house is across the farm road, connected to its own garden by a wooden footbridge over a bioswale. It is quite separate from the swimming pond and garden, which is a distinct destination on the 35-acre site.

The garden covers just two-thirds of an acre but contains a variety of spaces and structures—a bocce court is shaded by a row of river birch, adjacent to a dining terrace. Across a flagstone terrace, the fire pit has a view of the swimming pond, and the outdoor shower is tucked out of sight and around the corner, nestled amid oakleaf hydrangea, Virginia sweetspire, and sweetbay magnolia.

The space relates to two buildings—an apothecary/greenhouse, where the owner works with the herbs and plants for her holistic medical practice, and the library/office.

A focal point in this multifunctional garden is the natural "swimming hole," which doesn't require chlorine to maintain water quality. Instead, a filtering system keeps the pond functioning as an environment for people and wildlife.

Both support a functioning landscape—the owners offer retreats in nature—reminiscent of the gristmill that once operated on the site. The buildings' pitched roofs and cedar siding fit in with the farm landscape. This complex design developed over two years as the clients and the designer grew to understand the site's opportunities and how they wanted to live in and use the garden.

The garden is centered on the swimming pond. Like any suburban in-ground pool, it is dug into the earth, has a liner, and is fenced to meet code. But unlike most swimming pools, the circulated water is skimmed for large sticks and leaves and then naturally filtered using a biologically based system of filter media, beneficial bacteria, and plants.

The pool winters over without a cover, and Barnard speculates that you could skate on it when it freezes in the winter. It requires some maintenance, but "it's just like maintaining a garden," he says—cutting back some plants, adding others, and cleaning out debris.

This type of pool is unusual in the US. After consulting with other firms, he designed it on the site and worked closely with the contractor. The pool liner is topped with river stone and pebbles and edged with plants that both shade the water to discourage algae growth and create a natural transition to the surrounding stone terrace. The palette of more than twenty pond plants was chosen to thrive at different water depths—from 3 to 18 inches, with

some submerged. Swimmers enter through a shallow pebbled beach that leads to the deeper pool. A carefully chosen diving stone stretches out into the pool's deep end.

That diving stone is not something you can order off the shelf. "You have to go see it, to make sure you get the right one," Barnard says. He wandered around the quarry, described what he was after, and found the piece of stone that would work. This intuitive approach extends to the garden design and plant materials. Barnard sought to create communities of native plants that would define spaces and views, and that would also create habitat.

This natural approach makes sense in the Chesapeake Bay region, where critical area laws require setbacks from tidal waters, limits to impervious surfaces, and mitigation with planting. This approach is second nature to Barnard. "We are part of the food chain," he says. "Why mess around with the birds, plants, and insects that are part of it?" He views landscape design as an opportunity to maintain or return some of the natural habitat—an approach that fits the client and the site.

PLANT LIST

TREES

River birch, *Betula nigra*
Sweetbay magnolia, *Magnolia virginiana*
Loblolly pine, *Pinus taeda*
Pignut hickory, *Carya glabra*
Hackberry, *Celtis occidentalis*
American holly, *Ilex opaca*
Eastern red cedar, *Juniperus virginiana*
Black gum, *Nyssa sylvatica*
Sycamore, *Platanus occidentalis*
Scarlet oak, *Quercus coccinea*
Willow oak, *Quercus phellos*
Sassafras, *Sassafras albidum*

SHRUBS AND GRASSES

Red chokeberry, *Aronia arbutifolia*
Black chokeberry, *Aronia melanocarpa*
Coast azalea, *Rhododendron atlanticum*
Buttonbush, *Cepholanthus occidentalis*
Dwarf fothergilla, *Fothergilla gardenii*
Oakleaf hydrangea, *Hydrangea quercifolia* 'Snow Queen or Alice'
Bushy St. John's wort, *Hypericum densiflorum*
Inkberry holly, *Ilex glabra*
Winterberry holly, *Ilex verticillata*
Winterberry holly, *Ilex verticillata* (male)
Virginia sweetspire, *Itea virginiana*
Southern bayberry, *Morella ceracifera*
Northern bayberry, *Morella pensylvanica*
Switchgrass, *Panicum virgatum* 'Shenandoah'
Fragrant sumac, *Rhus aromatica*
Elderberry, *Sambucus canadensis*
Smooth witherod viburnum, *Viburnum nudum* 'Winterthur'
Blackhaw viburnum, *Viburnum prunifolium*

AQUATIC PLANTS

Marsh hibiscus, *Hibiscus moscheutos*
Cardinal flower, *Lobelia cardinalis*
Wool grass, *Scirpus cyperinus*
Iron weed, *Veronica noveboracensis*
Seashore mallow, *Kosteletzkya virginica*
Tussock sedge, *Carex stricta*
Sweet flag, *Acorus americanus*
Blue joint grass, *Calamagrostis canadensis*
Blunt spike rush, *Eleocharis obtusa*
Blue flag iris, *Iris versicolor*
Three-way sedge, *Dulichium arundinaceum*
Bog bean, *Menyanthes trifoliata*
Monkey flower, *Mimulus ringens*
Water plantain, *Alisma subcordatum*
Pickerelweed, *Pontederia cordate*
Lizards tail, *Saururus cernus*
Soft-stem bulrush, *Scirpus tabernaemontani*
Golden club, *Orontium aquaticum*
Arrow arum, *Peltandra virginica*
Water lily A, *Nymphaea* 'Virginalis'
Water lily B, *Nymphaea* 'Virginia'
Lotus, *Nelumbo* 'Beautiful Dancer'
Carolina fanwort, *Cabomba caroliniana*
Brazilian waterweed, *Anacharis*

ARCHITECTS: Kevin Shertz, Jennifer Lieber
BUILDER: Ben Herr
FABRICATION: Parker Welding (pool bannister), Steve Shumaker (handrail)
POOL DESIGN AND INSTALLATION: Ben Herr
SPA: Zen Bathworks
NATIVE PLANTS: Environmental Concern
AQUATIC PLANTS: Kelly Billing, Lilypons Water Gardens
PLANT MATERIALS: Anthony's Flowers and Landscaping, Tideland Gardens
STONE: Hepco Quarries
PHOTOGRAPHY: Allen Russ

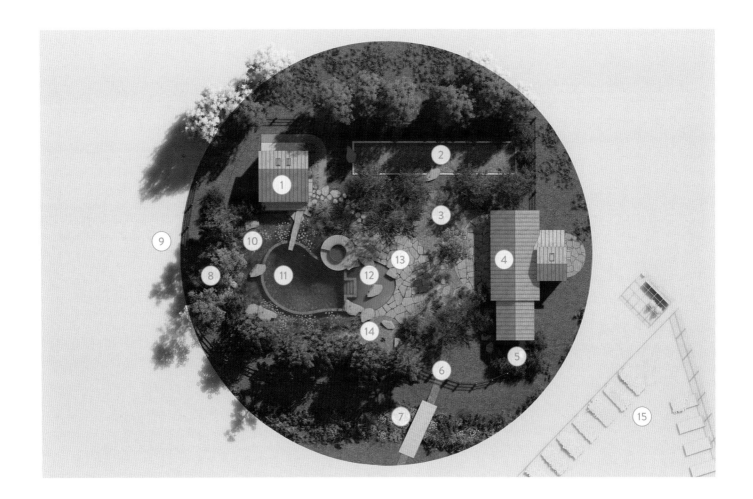

1   Library
2   Bocce court
3   Dining terrace
4   Apothecary
5   Outdoor shower
6   Garden gate
7   Bioswale
8   Native plant border
9   Meadow
10 Filter zone
11 Swim zone
12 Beach entry
13 Fire pit
14 Lounge area
15 Vegetable garden

Claudia Kousoulas is a freelance writer and editor whose work focuses on design, architecture, urban planning, and culinary history. She worked for more than 20 years as an urban planner in the Capital region, incorporating its particular historical and environmental character into her work. She is the author of *Contemporary Architecture in Washington, DC*; *Bread & Beauty: A Year in Montgomery County's Agricultural Reserve*; and *A Culinary History of Montgomery County, Maryland*. She lives in Washington, DC.